Local Government Briefings

The Case for Local Government

The Case for
Local Government

GEORGE JONES

London School of Economics and Political Science

and

JOHN STEWART

Institute of Local Government Studies, University of Birmingham

London
GEORGE ALLEN & UNWIN
Boston   Sydney

George Allen & Unwin (Publishers) Ltd,
40 Museum Street, London WC1A 1LU, UK

George Allen & Unwin (Publishers) Ltd,
Park Lane, Hemel Hempstead, Herts HP2 4TE, UK

Allen & Unwin, Inc.,
9 Winchester Terrace, Winchester, Mass. 01890, USA

George Allen & Unwin Australia Pty Ltd,
8 Napier Street, North Sydney, NSW 2060, Australia

First published in 1983

British Library Cataloguing in Publication Data

Jones, George
  The case for local government.
1. Local government–Great Britain
I. Title   II. Stewart, John
352.041   JS3173   ·
ISBN 0-04-352107-X
ISBN 0-04-352108-8 Pbk

Library of Congress Cataloging in Publication Data

Jones, G. W. (George William)
  The case for local government.
Bibliography: p.
Includes index.
1. Local government–Great Britain. 2. Decentralization in government–
Great Britain. I. Stewart. John David, 1929-   . II. Title.
JS3137.J66 1983   352.041   83-15852
ISBN 0-04-352107-X
ISBN 0-04-352108-8 (pbk.)

Set in 10 on 11 point Times by Fotographics (Bedford) Ltd
and printed in Great Britain
by Billing & Sons Ltd, London and Worcester

Contents

Acknowledgements

The following chapters are based on material originally printed in the listed publications. We thank their editors and publishers for allowing us to use them as the foundation for chapters in this book.

1 J. W. Raine (ed.), *In Defence of Local Government*, Institute of Local Government Studies, October 1981.
2 *New Society*, 25 February 1982; and *Local Government Chronicle*, 18 June 1982.
3 *Local Government Studies*, January/February 1982.
4 *Local Government Studies*, May/June 1982.
5 Raine, *In Defence of Local Government*.
6 *Municipal Journal*, 21 May 1982.
7 *The Political Quarterly*, January–March 1983.
8 *Local Government Chronicle*, 21 May 1982; Raine, *In Defence of Local Government*; *Municipal Journal*, 14 May 1982.
9 *Local Government Chronicle*, 2 April 1982.
10 *Education*, 30 July 1982.
11 George Jones, John Stewart and Tony Travers, *The Way Ahead for Local Government Finance*, Institute of Local Government Studies, March 1982; *Municipal Journal*, 2 July 1982; and *Local Government Chronicle*, 8 January 1982, 22 October 1982 and 19 November 1982.
12 Jones, Stewart and Travers, *The Way Ahead for Local Government Finance*.
13 *Municipal Journal*, 5 June 1981 and 10 July 1981.
14 *Social Policy and Administration*, Spring 1982.

Postscript   *The Guardian*, 26 June 1983.

Introduction

This book is a polemic. It is based on a series of articles and papers written by the authors in defence of local government against attacks of recent years.

We have amended the original publications, up-dated certain figures, eliminated some overlap, filled some gaps, but have left the basis of the material untouched. The present tense and the impression of tackling current conflicts are unchanged. The book was formed in controversies of the moment, and we do not want to conceal or temper that immediacy in retrospective safety.

For the future, we feel it is not sufficient just to defend local government. Too much damage has now been done to local government for us to be content with present confusions and instability. The book therefore ends with a new paper in which we put forward a new framework for local government. That has become our fresh objective and the purpose of this book.

The book is our own in all its controversy. We are grateful to those colleagues who have joined us in particular parts of the book – David Regan, Francis Hill Professor of Local Government, University of Nottingham, Royston Greenwood, Senior Lecturer, Institute of Local Government Studies, University of Birmingham, and Tony Travers, Research Fellow, North East London Polytechnic. We are grateful to those editors who have printed our articles and have now given us permission to reproduce them – the *Local Government Chronicle, Local Government Studies, Social Policy and Administration, Municipal Journal, Education, New Society, The Guardian* and *The Political Quarterly*. We are grateful too to the many academic colleagues, officers and councillors from local government who have encouraged us. We must acknowledge also those ministers and civil servants whose centralising activities have provoked us to embark on our campaign.

The book reflects our belief that local government is a vital part of our constitution, worth defending and worth reforming so that it can fully realise its potential as a major component of truly democratic government.

Part I

Local Government Analysed

1 The Case for Local Government

Introduction

The crisis in the relationship between central and local government continues. Since 1979 – as in previous governments – ministers have sought to increase their control over local authorities but the pace of centralisation has increased. Bill followed bill; bills were introduced, only to be withdrawn or heavily amended; proposals were put forward only to be jettisoned and succeeded by further proposals; and all the time no fundamental and long-term solution was undertaken – short-term palliative followed short-term palliative. The message of central government was that it needed to control disobedient local authorities. Its measures and proposals were designed to increase centralisation and to weaken local government. By July 1982 one minister (Leon Brittan) was openly questioning the case for local autonomy over priorities and in the administration of services. The very existence of local government appeared under serious threat.

The need is to look beyond any short-term crisis and panic measures, beyond the immediate attack and the consequent defence, to a long-term and positive solution. The continuing crisis has destabilised central–local relationships and has undermined local accountability. Already in three years local government has been subject to seven grant systems. Local authorities' finance has become more dependent on the vagaries of grant mechanisms, changing almost every six months, than on their own policy decisions. The process of *ad hoc* change followed by *ad hoc* change has resolved nothing, but eroded further a sense of local responsibility. Stability will and can only be restored by a new settlement that strengthens local accountability. Such a settlement involves consideration not merely of local government finance but of the role of local government itself in our society.

This book considers, therefore, not only the short-term problems of the present, but arrangements for the long-term future of local government. A new settlement is required if local government is to be re-established on a foundation that can last for the rest of the century. That settlement must include finance and functions, structure and role. Events of the last few years have made a new basis for local government imperative; but it should be determined by the needs of the future and not by the crisis of the present.

The case for local government is strengthened not weakened by the crisis and the challenges that face British society and the British economy. That is not the common response. As crises grow and as challenges deepen, the approach most commonly advocated is to increase the power of the centre over the locality. Central government tries to strengthen its fortress against the uncertainties of a troubled world. This defensive policy may be the natural response, but it is not necessarily the right one. An increase in central government power may, far from being the right response, actually reduce the ability of our system of government to resolve the problems it faces.

To centralise is to reduce the learning capacity of the system, because possibilities are sifted out as they mount the hierarchies of decision-making. To centralise is to reduce the adaptiveness of the system, as organisational scale and complexity increase, and the responsiveness of the system, since issues are dealt with according to rules determined in settings remote both geographically and organisationally from the problems they tackle. To centralise in government may appear to strengthen its power, but it may well weaken the ability to use that power effectively.

The apparent weaknesses in our system of government may not in fact be due to a lack of centralisation, but to over-centralisation. The machine at the centre is already over-burdened by the problems of localities. The unnecessary handling of these problems by national government may prevent it from dealing adequately with those problems which can be dealt with only at the centre. What is required is not a strengthening of the centre, but a re-structuring of government that increases the capacity of local government, while leaving for the centre the roles and power appropriate to its tasks. The need is not to aggregate unnecessarily problems so that the solutions become larger in scale and yet more difficult to achieve, but to disaggregate problems so that they are more manageable and within the range of local capacity.

Central government has a concern with many of the issues dealt with by local authorities, but that concern should be with the broad framework within which local authorities operate, setting their powers and duties, the overall national objectives for their services and the equalisation of resources. The aim should be to enable local authorities to enjoy policy discretion that goes far beyond the mere administration of services. Wherever central government has to determine some aspect of local government, then legislation, not ministerial regulation, should establish the framework for local government action. There should be no need for continuing interventions by ministers with their destabilising effects.

The case for local government is not made on behalf of the present structure and functions of local authorities, or for their present management and organisation. It is made not to support the present form of local government, but to enable that form to be reconstructed. The case is made for the potential of local government, as separately elected authorities exercising legitimate power over a wide range of functions within a defined geographical area. The task for local government is to realise that potential.

The Diffusion of Power

Local government is no passing luxury. It should be a guardian of fundamental values. It represents, first and foremost, a spread of political power. Power is diffused among many different organisations. Local authorities are, however, the only institution other than the House of Commons within the country that can claim the authority that comes from election. Local authorities can represent the dispersion of legitimate political power in our society.

As the Layfield Report said (1976, p. 299), perhaps the most important issue is 'whether all important governmental decisions affecting people's lives and livelihood should be taken in one place on the basis of national policies; or whether many of the decisions could not as well, or better, be taken in different places, by people of diverse experience, associations, background and political persuasion'. Local government is grounded in the belief that there is value in that spread of power and in the involvement of many decision-makers in many different localities.

Diversity and Difference

There is not merely virtue in the spreading of power and the involvement of many decision-makers in governing, there is strength in diversity of response. Needs vary from locality to locality, and the richness of that variety can rarely be captured in the uniformity of national standards of provision. Not only do needs vary but so too do the aims and wishes of those who live in different areas. The local authority provides the means of expressing that difference in values. The local electoral base legitimates the capacity for difference. That capacity creates the opportunity for innovation and experiment and is the start of social learning. There is thus a positive value in diversity. We do not live in a society so certain that it has achieved the right solution to the massive problems of urban and rural areas that we can afford to risk the uniformity of single national solutions.

Diversity is an important element in social learning. From the uniformity of standard provision or of grant-related expenditure targets, little can be learnt except that which is already known. Social learning can come from the actions of different local authorities with different patterns of provision, experimenting, pioneering and carrying out their services in different ways. They can learn from their own efforts and from those of other authorities. Indeed, the great strength of local government should be that it promotes efficiency, by providing services, and a mix of services, that better fit local conditions and circumstances than can ever be achieved by more distant decision-makers.

The Localness of Local Government

Local government is local. Some would regret that it is not more local. Yet the local authority is still a *local* authority. Its actions mainly affect a limited area. Its headquarters may be very close to many of those affected by its services – rarely more than an hour or so away. Its officers and councillors live close to the decisions they have to make, to the people whose lives they affect, and to the areas whose environment they shape.

Decisions are made about situations known and seen by at least some of those involved in the decisions. Such knowledge should be a safeguard against the abstractions of decision-making, which can prevail when decisions are taken at a distance. The local authority has the potential by reason of this localness to be accessible and exposed to influence by its citizens. Its activities and decision-making processes should be more visible than those of the great departments of state. It operates on a scale that can be seen and comprehended, and makes it vulnerable to challenge. This visibility makes it open to pressure where its activities fail to meet the needs of those who live and work in its area.

There is a growing demand for decisions to be taken closer to those affected by them. The strength of local government is that it provides the potential to satisfy this aspiration. Localness should be the basis of responsiveness in local government. Indeed, the great strength of local government is that it can provide democratic public control over bureaucracy in organisation far more effectively than can be achieved in large national bureaucracies headed by ministers or appointed boards.

The Political Economy of Local Government

Resources can be much better matched to the diversity of needs and wants by the decisions of local authorities than by the application of national standards. The search for objective measures of need, whether pursued through the statistical complexity of regression analysis or the pretensions of grant-related expenditure (GRE) factors which hide political and value judgements in formulae, is a misleading enterprise. Judgement of need can be better made by those close to the reality of local circumstances.

That judgements vary from local authority to local authority is not to be regretted but welcomed. Local judgement of need should be a better basis for economy than a uniform application of national standards. True economy lies in the matching of local resources and local needs. If that key element of the financial system is yet further weakened, the basis for economy is removed.

The case for local government is also that it can sustain the notion of community government, which is especially valuable when the concept of public provision is under attack. The growth of government has entailed higher taxation to finance the extended role of collective services. In a time of plentiful resources, voters were prepared to pay higher taxes for better governmental provision, but in an era of scarce resources, squeezes and cuts, they tend to put their private interest in reduced taxation before the provision of community services. They are encouraged to do so when services are increasingly determined by central government, because the public find it difficult to see the connection between the taxes they pay and the services they receive. Through local government, however, the citizen is able more easily to perceive that linkage and thus more willingly to pay taxes and support collective provision and community values. If central government insists on enhancing its own role in the provision of services, its demands for taxation are likely to alienate more and more people from the idea of public services and to encourage them to make more private provision. Individualistic self-seeking and private consumption will be stimulated at the expense of community welfare. Local government, by making government less remote and more manageable, makes it more comprehensible, enabling a clear and balanced choice to be made over the extent to which people wish to promote community values.

So, to meet the complex challenges of our time our system of government must have the capacity

- to learn,
- to respond,
- to change, and
- to win public loyalty.

Our argument is that learning is advanced by a diffusion of power and a diversity of approach, because there is more to learn and greater variety to learn from. Centralism reduces the capacity of learning.

Our argument is that localness brings a capacity to recognise and to respond to problems and issues, because decision-making in the locality is about situations known and is itself more open to pressure.

Our argument is that change comes more easily in organisations on the smaller scale and can be achieved with greater economy, because it is matched to local need.

Our argument is that through local government the public is more easily able to perceive the linkage between taxation and public expenditure, and thus support community provision.

A centralised system of government would have a reduced capacity to learn, to respond, to change and to win the support of the public. Our case is for strong local government.

Our argument is based on the potential of local government compared with central government for the tasks and roles with which we are concerned. Potential is not always realised in practice. Our concern is to establish an approach to local government that will assist the realisation of that potential.

The Alternative to Local Government

We are not so foolish as to argue that all is well in local government. There are inefficiencies in local government, local authorities that are unresponsive to local pressures, and local bureaucracies that pursue their own interests. But even where such accusations are made, and justifiably so, they are made because of the very visibility of local government. There is no Official Secrets Act guarding even routine decisions from public scrutiny. Committees of local authorities generally meet in public and their agendas are open in ways that would horrify civil servants or central government politicians. Local councils publish information about their performance in ways that central departments show no sign of emulating for their central, regional and local offices. Local government is more subject to public challenge through the courts, to a public and searching audit and generally to public investigation than any department of central government. The system is open and provides thereby correctives to revealed defects.

Those who are concerned about the defects of local government should worry deeply about the only alternative that is on offer – centralism. The alternative to local government based on present principles is government either by central government or by appointed authorities dependent on central government. Even those who are anxious about the efficiency and accountability of local government should be wary about any increase in the power of central government. It would lead to a dangerous concentration of power in central government which would be able to decide not merely those matters directly under its control but also the expenditure of each and every local authority or whatever body might eventually replace them. Not, as now, would there be at least some counter-balancing views on local expenditure, but central government would be able to enforce its views on the wide range of public expenditure for which it was responsible and on the expenditure of individual authorities.

Concentration of power is a danger to a free society. A balance of views in action can temper extremes of policy. Concentration of power would also be centralisation of decision-making. Decisions on expenditure levels would no longer be made by many local authorities but by one central government which would be both organisationally and geographically removed from the areas to which the decisions were to be applied. Such decisions are likely to be made not in response to local perceptions of needs and wants but either – if experience of recent years is a guide – by setting arbitrary targets based on a previous year or by the complex formulae of GREs.

The movement of decision-making from local authorities to central government means the movement of decisions from a visible local bureaucracy to a largely invisible central bureaucracy, from control by councillors close to their officials – and involved in the affairs of their localities – to control by civil servants who can inevitably be only occasionally controlled by their political masters, the ministers. As the Secretary of State has said: 'I believe that an effectively functioning local democracy can monitor the activities of local councils far better than civil servants at Marsham St.'[1]

Nor is such change likely to lead to economy in the use of resources. There is waste in national standards of provision which bring authorities to levels of expenditure not sought by the local community. Such standards are a crude basis for the use of resources. Limitations on local authorities' responsibility for their own expenditure decisions coupled with an increase in central government's responsibility moves power from local authorities to central government. Such a step could mean:

- a dangerous concentration of power in central government;
- a movement of key decisions from the local level to national level, far from those on whom they have an impact;
- a strengthening of central bureaucracy with long anonymous and unaccountable hierarchies inevitable in large-scale organisations;
- the removal of many decisions from the direct political control that is possible at local level to control by civil servants;

- a decrease in the visibility and accessibility of government;
- an increase in uniformity at the expense of the diversity necessary for constructive social change;
- the replacement of responsiveness to local needs by national standards.

By contrast the general case for local government is that it embodies:

- diffusion of power in a society which cannot afford concentrating power in one central location;
- diversity of response in a society which cannot afford the centralist risk of single solutions which may go wrong;
- economy in resource utilisation in a society which cannot afford the waste of national standards unrelated to local perception of need;
- localness in knowledge and response in a society which cannot afford the remoteness, rigidities and limitations of centralised bureaucracy;
- democracy and self-government in a society which cannot afford to entrust control over bureaucracy to only twenty-one ministers and 650 MPs.

Note to Chapter 1

1   Department of the Environment, press statement: text of a speech by the Rt Hon. Michael Heseltine, MP, Secretary of State for the Environment, to the Society of Local Authority Chief Executives, 18 July 1979.

2 The Beliefs of Centralism

(with Royston Greenwood)

The movement to centralisation gains support from a set of beliefs that undermines local government. Beliefs are put forward as facts, and assumptions as certainties. The closed village that is Westminster and Whitehall, to which so many in Fleet Street attach themselves, reinforces these beliefs and assumptions, so that by constant repetition they come to seem truths, whereas they are no more than the assumptions and beliefs of a metropolitan elite that knows little of local government.

The centralist wisdom is that, in order to manage the economy, central government needs control over local government expenditure, and requires it even more today, because it is out of control. Two other strands in the case for centralism are: the public *expects* clear central control over local government; and the public, in any case, has little electoral commitment to it. All these beliefs are assumed, rather than proved. Central intervention has become one of the critical and untested assumptions of our government and our society. In this chapter we investigate four main fallacies, and question whether the centre is somehow politically and administratively better than local government.

Fallacy One: The expenditure record of local government justifies greater central control

Central government already has control over its grant to local authorities, because it is raised through national taxation. And it needs control over borrowing by local authorities, because it is concerned with the public sector borrowing requirement. But there is no clear case that central government needs control over that part of local government expenditure which is financed out of *local* taxation (such as rates). This sort of expenditure only substitutes public goods for private goods by local choice. It does not increase aggregate demand. It has no effect on the public sector borrowing requirement or on the money supply. There is thus no *economic* case for any control of local expenditure financed from local taxation.

Fallacy Two: Local government expenditure is out of control

What does this allegation mean? One interpretation is that the level of spending is increasing, but it is not true. Since 1975/6 United

Kingdom local government expenditure has fallen by 16.6 per cent up to 1980/81. Over the same six years central government expenditure has increased by 7.5 per cent. Under the Conservative government (i.e. since the 1978–9 financial year) local government spending has dropped 5.5 per cent over the two years to 1980/81. Spending by central government has gone up by 6.7 per cent.

In short local government spending is not out of control. On the contrary, you could say that *central* government spending is out of control. Certainly there is no evidence that the centre is better at controlling it. But you might say that 'out of control' did not refer to a rise or fall in spending. It could perhaps mean that current expenditure does not conform to the proposals and targets set by the government. This accusation does not stick, either. The evidence is that local authorities have traditionally stuck closely to the government's line. Thus:

- In 1975–6, spending was 0.3 per cent above target.
- In 1976–7, spending was 0.4 per cent *below* target.
- In 1977–8, spending was 0.7 per cent *below* target.
- In 1978–9, spending was 1.7 per cent above target.

These figures hardly suggest that spending was out of control. And yet it was *these* figures on which Michael Heseltine and Sir Geoffrey Howe based their conclusion that a new grant system was necessary in order to make authorities conform to central targets.

Switching Targets

Admittedly, the figures since 1978–9 are confusing (i.e. since the Thatcher government took office). But this is because the government has persistently changed the targets, as often as three times in one year. Nevertheless, it would appear that:

- In 1979–80, spending was 0.2 per cent below the Labour target, and 2.8 per cent above the Conservative target.
- In 1980–1, spending was 2.1 per cent above target.

The loud claims about lack of control are still not justified. Individual authorities are spending much more than the average target: but so what? The targets were meant as averages, and they were substantially achieved. To claim that they justify the new powers obtained and sought by the government is a deceit.

In the financial year 1981–2 local government as a whole seems to be over-spending the guidelines by about 5 per cent.

But this 'over-spend' still represents a fall in current expenditure of almost 3 per cent. Most observers would regard such a cut as a victory, not as a failure demanding constitutional upheaval.

Fallacy Three: The public expects central control because of:

(a) The need for uniform standards for services throughout the country

There is little evidence for this. If the public were asked whether they wished to have a common standard of services, they would probably say Yes. They would also say Yes if they were asked whether services should vary according to the wishes of local people and the needs of local areas. A 1980 Gallup poll showed that more (34 per cent) felt local government was not independent enough than those (17 per cent) who felt it was too independent.

Various polls between 1975 and 1982 showed that – faced with a choice of cutting taxes and rates, if it means a reduction of services, and increasing taxes and rates in order to extend services – more people favour higher taxes and widened services. The government's attempts to cut expenditure and taxation, and to impose a national standard, are not as popular as they are often assumed to be.

(b) The need to ensure minimum standards for services

Common standards for services have emerged more from the decisions of different local authorities than from the interventions of central government. Local authorities are themselves elected bodies, subject to the popular pressures of society. When there are pressures for common standards, local authorities will reflect them. If not, then not.

National minimum standards, either in statutes or in statutory instruments, are in fact rare. Most mandatory obligations laid on local authorities are general. They empower local authorities to perform certain functions and lay down procedures, but they leave them discretion about the level and extent of the services, their frequency and intensity. The standards which have emerged are not nationally determined and imposed minimum standards. They are common standards that have evolved, and continually develop, from a variety of pressures, political, professional and administrative, both central and local in origin (see pages 74–5, 81–3).

(c) The need to check bureaucracy and inefficiency

There are, of course, inefficiencies in local government. All large and complex organisations have inefficiencies. The question is: Are local authorities especially inefficient, compared to the centre? We doubt it.

There are two sets of forces that give evidence of relative inefficiency. First, there is the pressure on resources. Bodies undergoing cuts can be expected, other things being equal, to be more cost conscious, and more diligent in removing inefficiencies, than those where resources are less restricted. On these grounds, the centre is less likely to be efficient than local authorities. Take, for example, the following target figures.

Expenditure on the administration of roads and transport (1978–9 to 1981–2):

- Department of Transport: up by 3.7 per cent.
- Local government: down by 11.9 per cent.

Expenditure on housing administration (1978–9 to 1981–2):

- Department of the Environment: up by 16.7 per cent.
- Local government: down by 17.6 per cent.

There may be perfectly good reasons for the central increases. But, at best, they show the supposed better record of the centre, by comparison with local government, is not proven. At worst, they suggest that the move to centralism will increase inefficiencies.

The second set of forces is the existence of machinery which can *expose* inefficiencies. In this, local authorities are much more visible and open to scrutiny than the centre. Councillors and their officers provide services where they live and work and are known. So they are more susceptible to public criticism than central politicians and civil servants. There is no protection for the bureaucracy of the local authority through Official Secrets Acts.

Fallacy Four: There is little electoral commitment to local government because:

(a)   Local government and councillors are unpopular
The implication is that local authorities and councillors are more unpopular than any other part of government; that they are less trusted, more corrupt and more inefficient. In fact, the few polls that have been carried out show local councils to be more trusted than central departments. They are seen as more responsive to local needs.

Local authorities are not especially popular, efficient or responsive. But they are comparatively popular, efficient and responsive, when set beside central government. In many services, the critical choice is between administration by central government or by local government. Whitehall and Westminster cannot claim a wider basis of popularity, or more trust, than the town hall.

An NOP/MORI poll of 1973 asked respondents: 'Which two or three of these organisations best look after your individual rights?' and 'Which two or three of these organisations are most interested in ordinary people?' Local councils came top on both counts (36 and 33 per cent respectively), as against Parliament (18 and 6 per cent) and the civil service (4 per cent on both questions).

A 1978 survey by Louis Moss of attitudes towards government found that the tendency is to assign credit much more to those who perform functions locally than to government in London, and to assign blame much more to London than to local decision-makers or local workers. He found that satisfactory contacts with local offices far outweighed in total such contacts with any other set of public actors. His survey showed that all socio-economic groups select the local councillor as the one they would most trust. The local councillor was chosen by most people in all sections of the population as more likely than other actors to be trusted to look after your interests (Moss 1980, Chs 3, 6, 7 and pp. 328–30). This finding was in line with a 1974 Gallup poll, and the survey conducted in 1976 for the Houghton committee on financial aid to political parties.

A Gallup poll for *New Society* in 1982 showed that a majority disapproved of measures to increase the ability of central government to control the level of spending by local councils. A MORI poll of 1981 showed that 85 per cent believed that local councils were better placed than central government to decide how much needed to be spent in a local area.

(b)   The public look to MPs, rather than to local councillors
There is nothing more widely believed among civil servants and MPs than that the public complains to central government, rather than to local councillors. MPs claim that their mail bags are full of correspondence about local matters, and the few surveys of the correspondence of MPs do, indeed, show that their mail is dominated by local issues. But it is not merely a matter of comparing mail bags. A councillor lives in the area for which he is responsible. So he is subject to contacts, complaints and pressure throughout his working day and leisure hours in a way that would be impossible for many MPs, who live far from the areas they represent. The letter is only one of a multifarious range of contacts between the public and their councillors. The Louis Moss survey found that 45 per cent of respondents had had contact with local council offices, and 22 per cent with a local councillor. Only 14 per cent had contacted an MP.

(c)   Local government elections are solely determined by the popularity of a national government

National factors have a dominant effect upon local elections. But that does not mean local factors have *no* significant effect. In the local elections of May 1981, marked differences were noted in different parts of the country. But the only form of explanation was about north–south divides or the level of unemployment. It did not enter into the minds of most commentators that these results were from *local* elections, and that in some cases people were voting about the behaviour of their local councillors.

The few attempts to analyse local factors suggest that, at least in recent years, they may be becoming more important. The Centre for Environmental Studies found a relationship between rate increases and voting. As political division grows in local government, such local factors may count for more. We need more analysis of why, for example, Tameside in the 1978 local elections swung towards Labour, against the national trend; and why the Liberals often succeed in local elections in a way that is unrelated to national factors.

There is no clearer indication of the dominance of the assumptions and beliefs of the centre, mediated through press, television and radio, than the myth about local elections. The 1982 local elections were widely reported in the press, and were analysed as if they were national elections. The Falklands factor was assessed, the implications for the next general election considered, and academics discussed the swings on the basis of parliamentary constituencies, regional effects and consequences for the national parties. But these elections were local elections which produced local councillors. At least on occasion reference might have been made to that fact. One or two commentators mentioned that the results appeared to be uneven: there was an unexplained factor at work. The unexplained factor just could be that in *local* elections some voters are concerned with the performance of their *local* councils and councillors.

It is so readily accepted in the media that local elections are about national issues that the possibility that local issues influence, and are increasingly influencing, the results goes virtually unexamined. Because analysis is directed at finding uniformities, local variation goes unrecorded. But since the mid-1970s local factors increasingly influence the results and this important development strengthens local government and the case for local government. These issues can relate to the council as a whole and to the performance of the controlling party, or to ward issues, or to the performance of individual councillors. The existence of national trends cannot be denied, but they can be and are modified by local factors.

Local elections matter. Local parties may differ on important issues, such as expenditure, on whether cuts should be made and where they should be made, and on the rate to be levied. They differ in their approach to privatisation, in their attitude to public transport subsidies or charging, on rent policy and the sale of council houses. It is not surprising, therefore, that the local electorate vote in response to local circumstances.

Because of the widespread scepticism about the significance of local issues, the evidence needs to be stated. Full analysis requires research into the votes cast, but analysis of seats changing provides interesting indications. Local authorities in the same region showed very different results in 1982. In Wolverhampton, Labour made gains while in nearby Walsall Labour lost seats. Whereas in Bradford and Leeds Labour lost ground, in Barnsley they made large gains and in Sheffield maintained their position. In Rochdale, Labour lost seats, while in Oldham Labour gained seats. In Strathclyde Labour made gains but not in Lothian. The same type of analysis could be carried out for Conservative gains and losses.

Environment Secretary Michael Heseltine in his election broad-cast focused the attention of his viewers on a street in which houses on one side were in Lambeth and on the other in Wandsworth. He called upon the electorate to condemn the profligacy of Lambeth in contrast to the economy in Wandsworth. The electorate decided to condemn both. The Labour Party lost seats in Lambeth and the Conservatives lost seats in Wandsworth. The pattern of Alliance (or in particular Liberal) support showed considerable variation. The advance of the Liberal Party in Tower Hamlets from seven to eighteen seats or its emergence in Hackney cannot be regarded as the outcome of national factors, when the Alliance held only one seat in Islington.

Performance by a local councillor may be important. Where there was more than one councillor to be elected in a ward, there was often significant split voting. The voters discriminated between candidates of the same party.

It is not sufficient to identify differences in voting patterns; reasons must be found for the variations, and those reasons can only be understood in the context of the local political scene. For instance, it seems that the electorate were not reacting simply to left-wing or right-wing politics or policies. Differences in the result of left-wing councils in Lambeth and Walsall on the one hand and in Sheffield on the other may be differences less in politics and policies than in style and impact on the local electorate. Where local factors are important the electorate are probably judging the performance of the council in power, or of the councillor, more often than the promises of the opposition.

An election held now in the Greater London Council – whatever its results – would be a local election deeply influenced by the electorate's views about the Labour GLC's policy and practice. Those policies and practices are now known to the electorate. They may not have been in May 1981, however clearly they were stated in the manifesto. In this, local elections do not differ from national elections. That local elections should be influenced by local politics is to be welcomed. This is a justification for local government.

The salutary lesson is that local elections can matter and that the actions of a local authority, or its failure to act, can affect the election – even when a Falklands factor is at work. It is a lesson that the closed village at the centre has still to learn.

3 Policy-Making in Central and Local Government Compared

The Commons and the Council

Elections for the House of Commons can occur at any time within a five-year period when it suits the convenience of the prime minister and his or her government. For local government, election dates are fixed and cannot be manipulated for the advantage of the party in power. In most urban areas they take place every year, soon after the level of rates has been fixed. In parliamentary elections, national parties and issues dominate, so that fairly uniform swings of opinion are recorded over the whole country. In local government elections, and especially since resources began to be seriously squeezed in 1975, local issues have played a growing and significant role, with some localities registering swings very different from national trends. Local councils should, therefore, not be seen simply as inferior to or as mirror-images of the House of Commons. They can be regarded as more in touch with local public opinion, reflecting local views about policy, expenditure and taxation. They have their own distinctive electorates who have cast their votes increasingly about local issues, and a democratic legitimacy quite separate from that of the Commons.

In local government there are over 520 principal local authorities, about 26,000 elected councillors, and if one adds in the 70,000 parish and community councillors then the figure reaches about 100,000 elected members. In the Commons there are 650 elected MPs. Local government is also closer to the citizens of the country in terms of social composition. Surveys have shown that councillors are more representative of the community than MPs. The Commons contains less of a cross-section of the population than local government; for instance women and a wider range of social classes are better represented on local councils than in the Commons. Thus, the greater number of councillors, the smaller size of their constituencies, and their more socially representative character give them the potential to be closer and more responsive to the public than MPs can ever hope to be.

MPs, of course, have close contacts with their constituents, and their post-bags bulge with letters from the public, largely about local issues. But the councillor's contacts with his or her community are multifarious and continuous. Councillors normally live and work in the local authority they serve, unlike MPs who may make only occasional visits to their constituencies.

Elected Representatives and Bureaucracy

At the centre, executive power is conferred on ministers. The Commons is a watchdog, a debating chamber to expose and publicise, and the body to which the government is responsible. Thus, the majority of MPs are not involved directly in policy-making or in policy-implementation. In local government, executive power is conferred on the council as a whole, a corporate body, which exercises its responsibilities through committees. Thus each councillor can be directly involved in policy-making and in the control of policy-implementation by virtue of his or her membership of the council and of its committees.

Local government officials, unlike civil servants, serve not just a single minister, but a committee, including opposition members. In central government power is more concentrated in the hands of ministers, including the prime minister. Their will prevails. In local government, chairmen of committees cannot be so autocratic: they have to share power, first with members of their committee and secondly with the other chairmen and members of the policy and resources committee. Councillors, even from opposition parties, have rights of access to officials and to information unknown to MPs. Councillors visit, as part of the routine of their work, the schools, homes and housing estates for which they are responsible. They, therefore, make decisions about areas, institutions and people that are not mere names but are part of their experience. Thus in local government there is more scope for elected representatives to make an impact on policy-making. MPs who have served as councillors often express frustration at their lack of involvement in policy-making as back-benchers compared with their direct and significant contributions as councillors.

In central government departments the dominant officials in the policy-making process are generalist administrators. Specialists, those with professional education and training, skills and expertise, are 'on tap not on top', advisers to the generalists. Ministers receive departmental advice through the generalists who process the contributions of the specialists. The views of the latter reach the minister after being filtered and adapted, distilled and perhaps distorted, by the generalists. In local government departments specialists, rooted in a professional discipline, are on top and contribute their advice directly to their political masters, chairmen of committees and the committees themselves. The opinions of the specialists are not laundered or suppressed by generalists. There is, therefore, direct interaction between the specialist expert and his or her political controller. Policy-making in local government will thus not suffer from misunderstanding or shaping by generalists, who are mainly concerned with parliamentary, cabinet and departmental business. Sitting on top of the long bureaucratic hierarchies through which central government has to administer services, ministers and their civil service advisers can never be as close to the public, and as sensitive to the demands and needs of differing localities, as local councillors and officials.

Local officials are more public figures than remote and anonymous central civil servants. Their views are widely known through their reports publicly presented to committees and at times even speeches to their committees. They are publicly questioned by councillors, not occasionally as when a select committee of the Commons calls civil servants before it, but as part of the normal working of committees. They are frequently identified in the press, appear on local radio and TV, speak at public meetings and are active in the community life of the local areas they serve, and in which, or near to which, they usually live. They are thus closer, more visible and accessible to local citizens than any civil servant. They are, therefore, more responsive to local pressure from the public generally, from local groups and from elected members. Indeed, the last are able to exercise tighter control over their activities than an MP or minister over central civil servants.

Recent developments have tended to reduce political control over bureaucracy in central government and to increase it in local government. While the centre has sought, in the pursuit of so-called managerial efficiency, to remove functions from direct accountability to an electorate or elected representatives by means of 'hiving-off' and establishing quangos and appointed boards, local government has been developing structures and processes of corporate planning and management, and of area management, performance review and councillor–officer working groups which, when grafted onto the traditional system of executive committees, enable elected members to be involved in detailed decisions on implementation, to direct policy for services and to exercise overall control over the totality of services they provide to their locality.

In financial policy-making, budgeting, estimates and expenditure control, local government has developed more effective procedures than at the centre, which is one explanation for local government's better record in the control of expenditure. In national government, departmental policy-making proceeds without close co-ordination with Treasury concern for both expenditure totals and the raising of revenue to finance that expenditure. In local government these three aspects are more closely linked, through such devices of corporate management as the chief executive, management team and frequent interactions between finance and spending departments. In the House of Commons, while MPs can be involved through the Public Accounts Committee in the process of audit (after the money has been spent), they have no committees to focus on departmental estimates and expenditure. The new departmental select committees have broad terms of reference, including finance, but encompassing also policy and administration, and the work of 'associated bodies'. They have so far shown no inclination to act as financial watchdogs. A glaring gap in the procedures of the House of Commons is over control of estimates and expenditure. In local government councillors are deeply involved in such processes through policy and resources committees and their resource sub-committees, and through service committees which are constrained by the policy and resources committee. In the Commons estimates and expenditure are rarely discussed, the presentation of departmental accounts is confusing, obfuscating and does not facilitate MPs' comprehension or control. In local government, all councillors are supplied with full information and they frequently grapple with both the policy and detail of the estimates and expenditure in full council and in committee.

The Public

The citizen is far more informed about local than central government. Councillors and chairmen of committees are not bound by anything like the Privy Councillor's oath of secrecy or the doctrine of collective cabinet responsibility. There is no Official Secrets Act to impose silence on local officials and representatives. Council and committee meetings are normally open to the public and press. Central government ministers and civil servants show no sign of wanting to emulate this openness in their own procedures. They maintain the shroud of secrecy around cabinet, cabinet committees and inter-departmental committees and go to great lengths to prevent the public learning of the advice given by civil servants to ministers, and of the substance of intra-departmental discussions.

There is far more information available about the performance of local authorities than about the activities of central departments. Local authorities have to publish a considerable amount of information on the rate demand notice and in annual reports. Comparative statistics pour out in regular series of government tables and from those published by such professional associations as the Society of County Treasurers, the Chartered Institute of Public Finance and Accountancy and the Rating and Valuation Association. Again, the centre shows no sign of publishing such data about its own performance, by, for example, sending each taxpayer information equivalent to that sent to the ratepayer by the local authority.

As Michael Elliott (1981) has pointed out, it is easier for the public to use the courts to challenge local government than for them to bring judicial action against the centre. Ratepayers have an automatic right of standing against local authorities as long as their claims are not frivolous: there is no similar right for taxpayers seeking redress against central government. The courts have devised procedures that enable individual and group rights to be more protected against local than central government. The constraints of natural justice are used more against local authorities than central departments. The 'reasonableness' of local government's decisions can be more easily challenged than can the decisions of the centre. The notion of 'public interest privilege', formerly 'Crown privilege', whereby the government can claim that certain information relevant to a case should not be produced in court, is not available for local government.

The individual citizen can be more involved in the financial administration of local than of central government. Both ratepayers and taxpayers may challenge assessments of their tax liability but the ratepayer may also challenge the assessment of other ratepayers, while the taxpayer has no such right in relation to national taxation. The accounts of a local authority, and the auditor's report on them, must be publicly displayed for individual inspection. The citizen may question the auditor, challenge items of expenditure he or she regards as suspect, and insist that the auditor state why he has not acted in respect of such accounts. The citizen may also ask the courts for a declaration that the item of expenditure was improper. But the citizen would find it hard to understand the national accounts, even if they were obtainable – not an easy operation. It would be difficult to scrutinise them. That duty rests with the Comptroller and Auditor General, and the citizen cannot initiate proceedings against him or the suspect-spenders.

Many of the functions of local government have rights of public participation built into them, for instance to express their views at public inquiries on planning issues, such as slum clearance and compulsory purchase orders and structure plans, and to be involved on boards of school governors – but above all the scale of local government and its closeness to the community render it accessible to influence by a variety of local groups on tenants' rights, environmental issues, public safety and social welfare to a far greater extent than can be possible in central government.

Conclusion

A comparison of the policy-making processes of central and local government thus reveals that local government possesses considerable advantages, which would be lost if central government were substituted for local government. Local government is more representative of its community than central government, and its representatives have more control over policy-making. They are brought into direct contact with specialists and professional officials, who are themselves more visible and responsive to the local community than their central counterparts. The structure and processes of local government policy-making enable elected representatives to direct both policy and administration, including finance, to meet local needs and conditions. Local government is also open to its public, who are provided with much information about the activities and performance of their local authority, and have many opportunities to participate in the policy process themselves and to challenge decisions they dislike through the courts and at audit. A shift of functions and responsibility to central government would destroy major democratic checks on bureaucracy. The public, MPs and ministers would be unable to ensure that the greatly enhanced central bureaucracies, with their extended and complex hierarchies, would be subject to effective democratic control. Bureaucracy would be rampant. The great strength of local government is that it subjects bureaucracy to tight control by representatives of the people and by the people themselves. That is why civil servants seem so intent on eroding and destroying local government.

The sound course is not to react to what are deemed local government errors by a Pavlovian call for more centralisation. It is to realise that much of the current unease and criticism arises because so much is known about the performance of local government. Because it is so visible it is more exposed to attack, while the centre is able to conceal its shortcomings in ways not available to local government. Where local authorities are said to have misbehaved, the solution is not to call in the centre to rap their knuckles and take over their role. Rather, the public locally should make use of the many channels that exist to constrain local councils to be responsive to their wishes.

Part II

The Continuing Crisis

4 The Layfield Analysis Applied to Central – Local Relations Under the Conservative Government

The Layfield Analysis

The period since the election of the Conservative government in 1979 has seen a continuing series of confrontations between central government and local authorities. The cause of the crisis lies in the problems and confusions identified by the Layfield Report on Local Government Finance, but the crisis has been deepened by the measures taken by central government over the period since 1976 and particularly by the actions of the Conservative government.

We stress the importance of a political analysis of central–local relations. The relationship between central government and local authorities is not between abstract institutions that can be relied upon to have clear objectives, perfect knowledge and to use policy instruments geared to those objectives, but they are organisations subject to many and often conflicting pressures, and whose key actors may be as likely to disclaim responsibility for their actions and to blame others, as to seek responsibility in order to achieve their goals. Such an analysis does not mean that it is impossible to structure the relationship between central government and local authorities so as to clarify responsibility, but that such a structuring must take account of the realities of political processes and pressures.

The analysis contained in Chapter V of the Layfield Report (1976) is first and foremost a political analysis of the conflicting pressures in the relationship between central government and local authorities. Thus:

> The 1960s saw a growing national political concern with the objectives and content of education, health, welfare, housing and transport services. This concern no doubt both reflected and affected the pressures in society for better services and for more uniformity of provision ... Not all the pressures were one way. There were and are pressures for more decisions to be made locally. (p. 65, para. 4)

While these pressures operated both centrally and locally, much of the impact was felt by the government. (p. 65, para. 5)

The heart of the Layfield analysis was that the financial arrangements generated pressures that sustained central rather than local responsibility.

> While there are political and social forces which encourage this trend, we have noted other pressures in our society for more local involvement in decisions. We have seen that, in the past, financial pressures seem to have been critical in tipping the balance of the forces towards the centre. (pp. 71–2, para. 21)

The factors in the financial arrangements which were stressed in the Layfield Report were the dependence of local government expenditure on a high level of government grant, the consequent concern of central government for the level of local government expenditure, and through the Public Expenditure Survey Committee (PESC) process a central government involvement in the breakdown of local government expenditure into its component elements. The high grant, the government's concern for the totality of expenditure, and its involvement in expenditure on particular services, served to create confusion as to where responsibility lay. Pressures for expenditure were felt as much by the government as by local authorities.

> The effect of increases in local expenditure, whether arising from improvement in services or increased costs of maintaining services, being regularly met to a large extent from national taxation, and of local authorities coming to count on this aid, is to weaken account-ability to local electorates. The sharp changes in the level of local taxation unrelated to local expenditure decisions which can occur with comparatively small changes in grant distribution when grants are high, have the same consequences. Under these conditions the decisions on the amount of grant and the distribution formulae come to assume crucial importance. At the same time the government seeks to secure a total level of local government expenditure in line with its economic planning objectives and to restrain the rise in rate poundages. It is therefore easy to see how local authorities come to request, and the government to provide, increasingly detailed specification of the extent to which expenditure on individual services, and the components of services, should be varied – and how Ministers, local authorities and the public come to regard this guidance as having overriding importance. But, continued over a period, the process destroys local accountability. (p. 72, para. 23)

There was thus a confusion of responsibility. Unless that confusion were resolved, 'Centralisation of expenditure decisions is the inevitable end to which a system depending on high and increasing grants, and associated with an inflexible and politically sensitive local tax, must lead' (p. 72, para. 25). For unless the confusion were resolved, there was no clear basis for local accountability.

Attempts to resolve the problem of the central–local relationship by 'a middle way' based upon partnership and increased consultation resolved nothing, because the confusion remained. Indeed, such measures added to the confusion by failing to clarify where responsibility and accountability lay. The Layfield Report argued that what was required was to separate the areas of responsibility of central and local government. Increased consultation without such a clarification merely emphasised areas of overlap and common concern, thus further confusing responsibility and accountability.

The Layfield Report stated that a choice had to be made between a financial system based on local accountability and one based on central accountability. The authors, along with the majority of the Committee, favoured local accountability. This choice involves far more than a change in the system of local government finance; but change in local government finance was involved. The Layfield Committee considered that a system of local government finance based on local accountability required:

- the removal of local government expenditure from the PESC process, thus lessening the concern of central government with the detail of local government expenditure, and
- the introduction of a new source of revenue (local income tax) to reduce the dependence of local government on central government grant.

The Green Paper issued in 1977 by the Labour government in response to the Layfield Report gave little sign of it having given serious consideration to the Committee's analysis. The starting point of the Green Paper was a reiteration of the rhetoric of partnership without any attempt to clarify the role of the partners.

> The Government accept that the dividing line between central and local responsibilities is not always clear. There are many reasons for this. The central/local relationship is changing all the time because national economic and social priorities can alter substantially even within quite short periods. It is not long, for example, since government policy encouraged rapid expansion in local services. Subsequent developments in the economy have meant restrictions on the growth of public expenditure in general and in the local government sector in particular. Nevertheless, the change in emphasis in the relative responsibilities of central and

local government remains compatible with a well understood and accepted constitutional relationship. Any formal definition of central and local responsibilities would lack the advantages of flexibility and rapidity of response to new circumstances. It would be likely to break down under the pressure of events. The Government's view is, therefore, that while clarification of responsibilities wherever practicable is desirable, a fundamental redefinition is not necessary as a basis for solving the problems of local government finance. The disadvantages of both the centralist and localist approaches are clear, and the Government do not think there is a case for the adoption of either.

The Government think that the minority of the Committee were right to emphasise the importance of seeking a middle way. But their particular solution is, in the Government's view, impractical. It is unrealistic to envisage developing a middle way which reduces the whole relationship between central and local government to a simply defined form of allocation of responsibilities. Rather the Government see the duties and responsibilities involved in the provision of local public services as being shared on a partnership basis between central and local government. Within this framework the balance of responsibilities will vary over time as circumstances change.[1]

Whereas the analysis of the Layfield Committee had shown the need to reduce confusion by separating the roles of central and local government, the Green Paper increased confusion by a re-assertion of the notion of partnership, but as the Layfield Report has shown, partnership was not shared responsibility but shared irresponsibility. It was not surprising that, having ignored the Layfield analysis, the Green Paper rejected the main recommendations of the Layfield Report. The Green Paper went on to recommend new controls over capital expenditure, the adoption of the unitary grant and a change to capital valuation as the basis of domestic rating, although these proposals were not in fact pursued by the government. In effect, therefore, the Labour government failed to take any significant action to deal with the main problems of local government finance.

According to the analysis of the Layfield Report, it was inevitable that in the absence of decisions clarifying the location of responsibility the drift to centralisation would continue. However, in the period since the 1979 election, the situation has changed much more rapidly than had seemed possible. Far from taking action to reverse the drift to centralisation, the government has taken a series of actions which have intensified the problems of local finance and have weakened yet further the basis for local accountability, without making the central government clearly accountable.

Three actions have eroded local accountability:

1   The assertion by the Secretary of State that there was a constitutional convention that targets set for local government expenditure had to be accepted by local authorities.
2   The specification by the Secretary of State of individual targets for particular authorities.
3   The destabilisation by the government of the relationship between central government and local authorities.

The New Constitutional Convention: Targets for the Total

The Conservative government has taken as its guiding principle an alleged constitutional convention which, it suggests, local authorities are breaking. The convention, as formulated by the government, is that local authorities should accept the targets for their expenditure as laid down by central government.

Tom King said in the House of Commons on 12 November 1981, 'every responsible local government leader, regardless of party, has made it absolutely clear that he accepts entirely the proper role of the Government in setting those overall expenditure targets'. This 'voluntary understanding' is now 'under threat from people who are no longer prepared to accept the basic tradition on which local government has stood – the acceptance of the Government's responsibility to set overall public expenditure targets . . .'[2]

In support of the existence of this convention, ministers quote past history under previous governments, when local authorities came close to the targets set by central government. However, in the 1960s and 1970s the language used was not the language of control. It was the softer language of being 'closely concerned'.[3] There was no assertion of a constitutional convention. In the published Public Expenditure White Papers from 1969 to 1975 figures for local government expenditure were expressed as tentative forecasts, very provisional and dependent on the outcome of rate support grant negotiations and the decisions of individual local authorities responsible for their own expenditure and levels of rates. If in practice local government came close to the level of expenditure expressed by central government, it was not because of a constitutional convention, but because the government used the policy instruments available to it, and because there was a widespread acceptance in local authorities that the forecasts for local government expenditure were necessary and could be achieved.

The government influences the framework within which budgetary decisions take place in local authorities. The most important feature of the framework that is under direct central government control is the rate support grant settlement. Within that settlement a symbolic importance attaches to the grant percentage, i.e. the level of grant as a percentage of relevant expenditure (even though it can be argued that the percentage over-estimates the extent to which local government expenditure is dependent on government grant), and the figures in Table 4.1 show how it has changed in recent years.

Table 4.1   *Grant Percentage at Main Rate Support Grant Order*

	England and Wales (per cent)	England only (per cent)
1975/6	66·5	
1976/7	65·5	
1977/8	61·0	
1978/9	61·0	
1979/80	61·0	
1980/1	61·0	60·1
1981/2	60·0	59·1
1982/3		56·1
1983/4		52·8

The Labour government had a major impact on the process of decision-making in local authorities, first because it reversed what had been until then an upward trend in the grant percentage, symbolising continuing growth in local expenditure year by year. The reversal of the trend in the 1976/7 settlement and the massive cut in 1977/8 both set a climate of financial constraint and created financial pressure on local authorities to rein in their spending. It was not surprising, therefore, that local authorities showed the restraint sought by central government. That change affected the climate of decision-making for the next few years, as indicated by the figures in Table 4.2.

Table 4.2   *Deviation Between Actual Change in Local Authority Spending and Guidelines*

Year	Guideline	Spending	Deviation
1975/6	+4·8	+5·1	+0·3
1976/7	0	−0·4	−0·4
1977/8	−1·0	−1·7	−0·7
1978/9	+1·1	+2·8	+1·7
1979/80	+1·6	+1·4	−0·2

The Conservative government elected in 1979 sought a new and further reduction in local government expenditure as part of its general policies on public expenditure. Yet it failed to use the main instrument available. The grant settlement for 1980/1, the first grant settlement for which the government was responsible, left the grant percentage unchanged at 61 per cent. Although the figure of relevant expenditure to which the percentage was applied represented a reduction, the unchanged grant percentage figure did not create a climate of restraint and cutback, and did not put local authorities under severe pressure. Although in later years the grant percentage was reduced, first to 59·1 per cent in 1981/2, then to 56·1 per cent in 1982/3 and to 52·8 per cent in 1983/4, the important point is that at the key moment of policy change in the 1980/1 settlement, the government failed to use the policy instrument that it had available and had been used by the Labour government.

The Labour government had also managed to persuade local government of the reasonableness of its guidelines. Its means of doing so was through full use of the Consultative Council but, and more importantly, its guidelines were seen to be attainable, and central government was seen, at that time, to be applying similar guidelines to its own expenditure

The Conservative government has not been able to achieve the same degree of acceptance of the reasonableness of its guidelines. The task facing a Conservative government in calling for restraint and cutback is inherently more difficult than for a Labour government. A Conservative government can find itself confronted by Labour local authorities totally out of sympathy with its calls for expenditure reductions. However, that is not a sufficient explanation of the difficulties the Conservative government has had in achieving adherence to its guidelines, since it faced severe difficulties from the outset, before electoral changes had brought Labour to power in many authorities. The reasons are twofold. The first is that the government made little or no attempt to persuade local authorities of the case for its guidelines. The best evidence of this neglect is that the government introduced its proposals for the control of local government finance, later embodied in the Local Government, Planning and Land Act of 1980, in the autumn of 1979, i.e. before the start of the first financial year which the new government could seriously hope to influence. We have already seen that, for that year, the government did not use the policy instruments it had available. We now see that far from attempting to persuade local authorities, it set out to obtain new powers over local government.

The other and more important point is that there was a widespread view in local government that the government was seeking a reduction in local government expenditure to an extent and at a pace that was unreasonable. Thus, after the Conservative government came to office in 1979, it replaced the Labour government guidelines of + 1·6 per cent by new guidelines of − 1·4 per cent, after the financial year had already begun. This reduction of 3 per cent was not likely to be achieved in the period allowed. In the year 1980/1 it sought a reduction of 3·7 per cent on the year 1979/80. The Conservative government was clearly seeking, and continued to seek, reductions of a scale well beyond that of the previous government. It faced, therefore, a much greater problem in persuading local authorities of the reasonableness of its views and yet, as we have seen, it put the emphasis not on persuasion, but on new legislation.

The record shows, therefore, that local government had conformed to previous guidelines, not because of an alleged constitutional convention, but because local authorities generally saw the government's guidelines as reasonable and because of the impact of the reduction in grant. The past record cannot be used to show the existence of a constitutional convention that local authorities have to accept the targets laid down by central government. Such a convention must be regarded as the brainchild of ministers.

It is difficult to see how such a convention could be accepted by local authorities, without undermining what had clearly been an accepted principle, written into the very statutory framework of local government – the right of a local authority within the law to determine its own level of expenditure as long as it is financed from its own taxes. If the alleged convention had existed, it would have implied that local authorities had to accept any guidelines, however unreasonable, set by central government, without regard to their own views. There is evidence that the criteria which central government applies to local government are more severe than the criteria it applies to its own expenditure (Raine, 1981, pp. 22–4 and 30–34). That is not surprising – a political analysis would suggest that a budgetary process which gave ministers the choice of meeting Treasury pressures for expenditure cuts, either by reducing local authority expenditure for which they are not directly responsible, or by reducing the expenditure of their own departments, is likely to result in targets for local authority expenditure which involve cuts, while central government expenditure will be maintained or increased – which is precisely what has happened, as the targets for current expenditure in Table 4.3 show, even after the exclusion of the social security programme.[4]

The unilateral promulgation of this newly found constitutional convention as the basis for action by the Secretary of State, coupled with a resource allocation process which biases the guidelines that are to provide the basis for the convention, have inevitably deepened the crisis in central–local relations. Local authorities have failed to meet the alleged targets by small amounts (by between 2 per cent and 3 per cent in 1980/1 and probably about 5 per cent in 1981/2 and in 1982/3). It would be hard to attach much significance to such relatively minor over-spending, were it not for the importance apparently attached to the alleged constitutional convention by which local authorities are obliged to meet, even to precise percentage figures, unreasonable targets arbitrarily thought up by the Secretary of State. The danger of this alleged constitutional convention is that it confuses even further where responsibility for local government expenditure lies, intensifying the problems identified by the Layfield Committee.

Table 4.3 *Total Current Expenditure (excluding the Social Security Programme)*

	1978/9 (actual)	1981/2 Plan	Change	% change
	(£m. at 1980 survey prices)			
Central government	31,088	32,411	+ 1,323	+ 4·3
Local government	16,911	16,112	− 799	− 4·7

Targets for Particular Authorities

A yet more fundamental change has been brought about by this government. Whereas previously governments stated general guidelines for local authorities, the Conservative government has introduced targets for individual local authorities, first in the Grant-Related Expenditure (GRE) Assessment produced under the Local Government, Planning and Land Act, 1980,[5] then in the volume targets laid down for the application of holdback penalties in the measures announced in the summer of 1981 and in the targets, based on both GRE and volume targets, set out as part of the rate support grant settlement for 1982/3 and 1983/4. The government has moved from a concern for the totality of local government expenditure to detailed targets for individual local authorities. Confusion has been further confounded as local authorities have been faced not with one target but with many, which may change even within the same financial year.

The change from the aggregate to the particular is of critical importance. The government in general and the Secretary of State in particular have involved themselves directly in issues that are at the heart of local accountability: decisions on the levels of expenditure in each and every authority. Two important consequences follow. The first is that pressures which have previously focused on the local authority will focus increasingly on central government. The more the government stresses its targets, and the more severe the penalties that it imposes become, the more important it will be for all those individuals and groups seeking reduced or increased expenditure in a local authority to put pressure on central government. The significance of the local authority will diminish, while that of central government will increase. The consequence is a major weakening of local accountability.

The second consequence is that central government in general and the Secretary of State in particular have put their own political prestige at stake on securing adherence by particular authorities to their targets. They have created a situation in which action by a local authority in determining its own level of expenditure can become a failure by central government. The central government then feels the need to increase pressure on that authority, or to take yet more powers to intensify this pressure. Centralisation is stimulated to expand but still under the rhetoric and guise of maintaining local accountability. The confusion identified by Layfield persists.

Up to now it has not been thought necessary for the government to state a view on the expenditure levels of individual authorities. The present government has decided that it must do so, and in doing so has added to the confusion in accountability. If local authorities are to be held to account by central government for meeting its targets, it is difficult to see the basis for local accountability.

The Destabilisation of Relations

Clear responsibility and accountability by public authorities require a stable framework within which the authority can operate. Without such a framework there cannot be a basis for local accountability. If the conditions under which an authority operates are continuously and continually changing, then its actions are likely to be determined as much by changes in conditions as by changes under its own control.

Local accountability for local government expenditure requires both a sense of accountability in a local authority, so that it regards itself as largely responsible for its own expenditure and taxation decisions, and a basis for those to whom the authority is accountable to assess how it has exercised its responsibility. The Layfield Report argued that a high grant level weakened local accountability, because critical local authority expenditure and rating decisions became more dependent on grant changes than on a local authority's own decisions on the level of expenditure and rates.

The actions of the present government have been to deepen this problem, as they have not merely changed the amount of grant, but the form of grant. Since the government was elected in 1979 at least seven different grant systems have applied:

1   The rate support grant system based on needs and resources elements, inherited from the previous government.
2   The system as under 1 above but with the 'transitional arrangements' penalties applied in 1980/1.
3   The block grant system based on grant related expenditure, introduced under the rate support grant settlement for 1981/2.
4   The block grant system with the holdback penalties based on volume targets, introduced in June 1981.
5   The block grant system with holdback penalties based on volume targets, but with exemptions for authorities meeting grant related expenditures, introduced in September 1981.
6   The block grant system with holdback provision related to a composite target based on GREs and volume targets and to GREs introduced in the rate support grant settlement for 1982/3.
7   The block grant system with holdback provisions related to composite targets, and the abolition of supplementary rates, under the Local Government Finance Act, 1982.

The history of the Local Government Finance (No. 1) and (No. 2) Bills in the 1981/2 session of Parliament illustrates the problem of instability. Each Bill represented an intervention in the relationship between central and local government to meet an immediate problem, but without regard to long-term effects. The relationship between two political institutions and their internal operations are complex. An intervention in these relationships has to be carefully considered, not merely for its short-term effects, but also for its long-term impact.

In the No. 1 Bill the proposal to introduce referenda as part of the budgetary process for all local authorities whose expenditure level was above an amount specified by the government was put forward to meet the alleged problem of over-spending by particular authorities. But it had much wider implications, and recognition of those consequences by government backbenchers led to the withdrawal of the Bill.[6]

The Local Government Finance (No. 2) Bill, later to become the Local Government Finance Act 1982, contained three main parts. The first part abolished the right of local authorities to raise a supplementary rate. The second part increased the powers of the Secretary of State to impose penalties on local authorities through the use of multipliers, and was retrospective in its coverage because of legal doubts about the powers of the Secretary of State to impose penalties on authorities which had not conformed with his targets for

1981/2. The third part provided for the appointment of an Audit Commission.

The Bill had to be significantly amended by the government. These amendments derived from back-bench concern about the effects of the abolition of supplementary rates and illustrate the dangers of proposals that do not take account of indirect as well as direct effects. The possibility of a supplementary rate gave flexibility to the working of the local authority, even though supplementary rates were rarely imposed. It meant that the budget as set at the beginning of the financial year did not have to take account of all contingencies, because there was always the safeguard of a supplementary rate. Abolition of the supplementary rate makes the original budget much more critical.

The series of issues that led to government amendments of the Bill concerned the right of the government to alter the principles on which multipliers were used to impose penalties after the budget has been made. Because of the abolition of the supplementary rate, such powers could have placed local authorities in a position in which they had no choice but to reduce expenditure. An unanticipated loss of grant could previously have been met by a supplementary rate. The abolition of the supplementary rate closed that option.

Although the government amendments have recognised the danger and have imposed restrictions on the extent to which such powers can be used, the issue goes much wider. Any actions taken by the government about the rate support grant after the budget has been made by a local authority have assumed a new significance, as has the accuracy of the inflation forecasts underlying the cash limits set on grant. The apparently simple action of removing the right of a local authority to raise a supplementary rate has had side-effects, precisely because it has reduced the capacity of a local authority to cope with changing situations.

We have dwelt on this instance because it is a critical example of destabilisation. A continuing series of changes leads to complex interactions, imperfectly understood. The basis of accountability is changed in ways that were not anticipated when the process began.

The Layfield Analysis Confirmed

The actions taken by the Conservative government have in effect intensified the confusion of responsibility and speeded up the drift to centralisation identified by the Layfield Committee. Far from clarifying the basis of accountability, it has confused it by asserting that local authorities have to meet guidelines set by central government, by laying down targets for individual local authorities and by a destabilisation of the financial base.

The government has not, however, opted clearly and openly for central accountability; rather it has acted to maintain the forms of local accountability, while weakening its basis. It has even asserted that it is enhancing local accountability, by the abolition or relaxation of about 300 central controls in the Local Government, Planning and Land Act, 1980 – controls that were minor and little used – whilst leaving other controls intact. It has justified the provision of more information to the public, the establishment of an Audit Commission and an extension of audit into value for money and comparative analysis as measures to promote the accountability of local authorities to their voters. Block grant and the referenda were similarly presented as strengthening local constraints on the decisions of local authorities.

Such measures have to be set in a political context and assessed in conjunction with the dominant political pressures at work. The prevailing political pressure was the central government's quest to ensure that local government expenditure conformed to the wishes of central government. These measures were put forward not to enable local authorities to be more responsive and responsible to local wishes but to enable the central government to get its way. In a different context, with a central government intent on promoting local responsibility, some of these measures might be seen as facilitating local accountability. These measures also reflect the confusion of responsibility identified in the Layfield Report. The government failed to clarify responsibility. Once again it muddied the waters, increasing confusion and ambiguity. But still, behind the rhetoric of a belief in local responsibility were actions that increased centralisation.

There is no clearer example of the extension of centralisation, whilst maintaining the forms of local accountability, than the legislation for Scotland. The Local Government (Miscellaneous Provisions) (Scotland) Act, 1981, gives the Secretary of State for Scotland virtually direct control over the level of a local authority's expenditure. (See Chapter 5, below.) It was feared that the government in England and Wales could exercise virtually similar powers under the Local Government Finance (No. 2) Bill, 1981, which removed local authorities' right to raise a supplementary rate. Clause 4 of the Bill as originally drafted appeared to give the right to impose penalties after the rate had been set, which would force local authorities to reduce expenditure. Again the government appeared to be attempting to take powers to control local government expenditure without clearly assuming responsibility. However, the government was again subjected to great pressure and later amendments appeared to go some way towards removing the danger of selective Scottish type mid-year grant reductions. Uncertainties remain and whether the danger has in fact been removed, events alone will prove.

The actions taken by the Conservative government have confirmed the analysis of the Layfield Report. Its actions have critically weakened local accountability without clarifying central accountability. As with the Labour government, the choice posed by the Layfield Committee has not been faced. That choice between local and central accountability still remains. The authors urge now, as when they signed the Layfield Report, that a choice should be made and that the choice should be in favour of local accountability.

Notes to Chapter 4

1   Secretaries of State for the Environment and for Wales (1977), *Local Government Finance*, Cmnd 6813 (London: HMSO), pp. 4–5.
2   House of Commons Debates, *Hansard*, 12 November 1981, Col. 743.
3   e.g. Chancellor of the Exchequer (1977), *The Government's Expenditure Plans*, Cmnd 6721 (London: HMSO), Vol. 1, p. 8.
4   Chancellor of the Exchequer (1981), *The Government's Expenditure Plans 1981/1982 to 1983/84*, Cmnd 8175 (London: HMSO).
5   The government has denied that Grant Related Expenditure Assessments are targets – presumably because if they did so they would encourage those authorities under the Assessment to increase their expenditure. However, by the actions the government has taken it has shown it regards them as targets, e.g. exempting from penalties local authorities whose expenditure is below the Assessment.
6   The proposals in the (No. 1) Bill were resisted not merely by the opposition and by those government back-benchers concerned at further restriction on local government's ability to determine its level of expenditure financed by the rates, but also by those government back-benchers who were concerned that the basis of local accountability in local elections was being undermined.

5 Developments in Scotland

The Local Government (Miscellaneous Provisions) (Scotland) Act 1981 is a constitutional statute of the first importance, yet under that title it passed through Parliament unchallenged and unnoticed by most MPs and by the national press.

The Act gives the Secretary of State for Scotland virtually direct control over the level of expenditure of each local authority. He can report to Parliament that there should be imposed on any local authority a reduction in rate support grant if he is satisfied that the estimated expenditure of the authority is excessive and unreasonable. No criteria are laid down as to how the Secretary of State will determine that the expenditure planned by the local elected representatives is excessive and unreasonable. No principles or guidelines are stated about how the Secretary of State should calculate the reduction of grant. The discretion of the Secretary of State is allowed free rein against the judgement of the local authority on its own level of expenditure and of local taxation – a judgement for which it is accountable to its own electorate.

This unfettered discretion – subject only to the normally automatic ratification by the government majority in Parliament – goes far beyond the powers laid down for England and Wales. In Scotland a local authority faced with a reduction in grant under this Act cannot raise a supplementary rate. Clause 18 of the 1981 Act provides that the local authority 'shall neither wholly nor partially offset the reduction (or anticipated reduction) with sums advanced from their loans fund' except in the unlikely event of the Secretary of State giving permission. In effect, therefore, the Scottish local authority, faced with a reduction in grant imposed by the possibly arbitrary judgement of the Secretary of State, has no way of replacing the lost income.

The argument is not theoretical. The Act has been used against the Lothian Regional Council, and against district councils. The scale of the grant reduction originally threatened against the Lothian Region in 1981 was immense. Its grant was to be reduced by £47 million – nearly three times the highest penalty suggested for English authorities. The equivalent of over a tenth of the possible penalty threatened for all English authorities was to be imposed on the Lothian Region, which, with a population of 750,000, is roughly equivalent in size and functions to a medium-sized English county. The reduction in grant of £47 million was almost 14 per cent of the Lothian Region's budget of £337 million. There was no possibility of balances or adjustments to fees and charges being able to meet such a massive reduction.

What is disturbing about the Scottish situation is not that the government can reduce its grant allocation – although there are strong arguments, both economic and managerial, against the withdrawal of grant on such a scale at such a late stage in the budgetary process – but that Scottish authorities in general have no means of replacing the lost income. The Lothian Council had no choice but to reduce expenditure, other than to continue its expenditure without the prospect of sufficient income to cover it for the full year – a perilous act.

The government has, therefore, in a cumbersome and indirect way taken power that is equivalent to the power of direction over local government expenditure. The only reason that the power of direction has been achieved in this confusing way has presumably been to conceal the fact that what is involved is a change of great constitutional importance. The very basis upon which local government exists, the very reason for its existence, has been destroyed. The Secretary of State is seeking to remove from selected authorities in Scotland the right (which still exists in England and Wales) to determine their own levels of expenditure as long as it is financed from their own taxes.

The process does not end with the Local Government (Miscellaneous Provisions) (Scotland) Act 1981. It was soon to be followed by the Local Government and Planning (Scotland) Act which adds to the Secretary of State's powers under the 1981 Act the power to limit rate increases in those local authorities found guilty 'of excessive and unreasonable' expenditure. With this Act the Secretary of State is seeking to remove from selected authorities the right to determine their own rates. If he feels the expenditure and rate levels of a particular authority are too high, he can order that any savings he effects should be returned to the ratepayers. He will decide their rate burden.

Major constitutional change has been introduced in Scotland to meet a particular financial situation. It is dangerous to erode institutions of government in such a manner and for such a purpose. The Secretary of State said that he regarded the expenditure of the Lothian Region as excessive and unreasonable. We have no doubt that if they had considered it, many Secretaries of State in Scotland, England and Wales would have judged the expenditure of particular authorities to be unreasonably high or unreasonably low. They have not done so because it has not been their business to do so. That is a matter for the local council and a local electorate.

The danger is that a principle once conceded may be extended. Parliament, virtually unknowingly, has accepted a change of massive significance – so far in Scotland only. That principle must be resisted in England and repeal sought in Scotland. For that principle undermines the right of a local authority to determine its own level of expenditure as long as it is financed by local taxation and to be accountable for it to its own local electorate.

6 A Pause to Consider the Position Reached

The period of office of the present government has been one of continuing change in local government finance and in the relationship between central and local government. It has been a time of continuing crisis.

That crisis is focused on one big issue – the right of a local authority to determine its own level of expenditure, as long as it is financed by its own taxes, a decision for which it is accountable to its own electorate. That right is at the heart of local government. It supports and ensures the basis of local choice. If that right did not exist, there would be no point in a local tax, since the objective of a local tax is primarily that it permits a local authority to make its own expenditure decisions provided it is willing to face up to their consequences in taxation.

The government's stance can be described as a formal acceptance of that right, coupled with its actual denial in practice. Because this right is so clearly fundamental to our local government system, it has not been directly attacked by the government in England and Wales, although, as we have seen, it has been attacked in Scotland. What the government has done in England and Wales has been to change the rules of the game so that it can so influence local expenditure decisions that it secures the results it wishes.

A most important feature of the government's actions is its expressed concern with the expenditure decisions of each local authority. Through all the changes brought about by the government, that concern has been constant, from the moment the critical change was introduced by the Local Government, Planning and Land Act of 1980. In that Act, as emphasised in Chapter 4, the government moved away from the policy of the previous government which was expressed in a concern for aggregate local government expenditure, to a concern for the expenditure of each local authority as expressed in the specification of a figure of grant related expenditure and in the power given by that Act to adjust the amount of grant according to the relationship between its actual expenditure and that specified level of expenditure.

This change from concern with the total to concern for the particular was critical because the government had involved itself in the local political process. It has argued that the change was in presentation rather than in substance, since equivalent figures for each local authority were implicit in the previous grant system. However, in a political process presentation is critical, since it provides the very basis of accountability. Whoever lays down the figures will be held responsible for their achievement.

From these figures for grant-related expenditure assessments (GREAs), the government identified certain authorities as over-spenders, because their expenditure exceeded GREAs. The identification of certain local authorities as over-spending was a clear intervention by central government in the affairs of particular authorities, for all it meant was that the judgement of a local authority about the need for the expenditure in its area (a judgement which it was elected to make) was different from the judgement of central government about the need for expenditure in that area (a judgement which it had not been elected to make).

If there are allegedly over-spending authorities, there are also allegedly under-spending authorities. Their existence is not a sign that there are dangerous forces at work. The danger would be if there were no over-spending or under-spending authorities, for that would be an indication that there was no point in local government. If every authority were to spend exactly what central government had laid down, there would be no point in a local authority, local taxes and local elections. There is no point in local authorities which make the same judgements as central government. Because of its implicit denial of that truth the government's specification of grant related expenditure assessment for each authority was so significant. But the specification of grant related expenditure was merely the first step.

The Local Government, Planning and Land Act, as passed, was based upon the concept of grant related expenditure. The difficulty for the government was that the assessment implied increases in expenditure for many authorities, while for other authorities it implied reductions in expenditure far beyond a level believed to be attainable in a single year. While it was uncertain what influence the implied targets would have on allegedly over-spending authorities, it was likely that those local authorities under-spending would increase their expenditure, because it would become more difficult to resist pressures for increased expenditure, when even a government committed to restraint in local government expenditure had identified them as under-spending.

The government therefore introduced targets for local authority expenditure which were based for the year 1981/2 on a 5·6 per cent reduction in volume terms on the expenditure in each authority for 1978/9. The government also announced the introduction of penalties for failure to achieve these targets. It was, however, forced to concede that these targets would not apply to local authorities which were not over-spending on their GREAs. The calculation of targets varied from year to year, taking different account of existing expenditure and of the relationship of expenditure to GREA, but still requiring a reduction of expenditure from all or virtually all authorities. The government continued to show a preference for targets rather than GREAs.

The existence of both GREAs and of targets was a product of the first step – the involvement of central government in the expenditure level of particular authorities. Having found that GREAs on which the Local Government, Planning and Land Act was based created new problems of expenditure control, targets were introduced and given increasing emphasis.

The rules of the game have been changed in the midst of the bugetary processes of local authorities prior to the financial year, and in retrospection even after the financial year was over. The Local Government Finance Act of 1982 contains a clause covering the use of multipliers which in effect gave legal authority for the use of penalties which had been announced for the preceding year. Grant system has replaced grant system. Complexity has been added to complexity. Targets and penalties have been grafted on to a block grant system based on grant-related expenditures and tapers. Thresholds and multipliers have been added to the jargon of centralisation.

The government has looked to such manipulation devices in the grant system to give them the same certainty as with direct control, and whenever it failed to do so they have changed the rules to increase the pressure on local authorities. They have in effect sought to give local authorities the freedom to do what central government wants. By so increasing the means of influence, in the end local government's right to determine its own expenditure becomes a mere formality.

A consequence of such perpetual change is that there is no clear measuring rod of the extent of change or of its limits. Local government can be undermined by incremental step succeeding incremental step without the cumulative effect of many changes or the critical effect of particular steps being recognised. As we suggest later in the book, a Charter for Local Government is required to provide such a measuring rod and set of limitations. In its absence we have to assess the position reached. The cumulative effect of change upon change has been severe. Responsible local government can be and has been eroded as surely and as much by continuing change as by direct assault.

If one considers the relationship between central and local government as at heart constitutional, since it is focused on the division of elected power in our society, then such a relationship requires stability. Stability does not rule out change, but change should be carefully considered and not continuously introduced – often at a moment's notice – to deal with what the centre sees as a financial problem. If there is to be responsible local government, the local authorities must know with certainty the conditions of that responsibility – the framework in which they are to operate. Yet the Local Government Finance Act passed in July 1982 changed the law as from April 1981. The rules of the game were changed after the match had been played. Continuing and even retrospective change has undermined the basis of responsible local government.

The erosion of responsibility caused by uncertainty was added to by the increasing incomprehensibility of the structure that had been created. For a grant structure to be understood its rationale must be clear and the various elements in the structure must be seen to derive from that rationale. The existing grant structure is not seen to have that clear rationale as various elements in the structure have been added on or adapted at short notice. In particular the combination of a grant system based on GREAs with penalties based on targets (sometimes in combinations with GREAs and sometimes at least threatened to be separate from GREAs) has no adequate rationale.

Figure 6.1 *The Relationship Between Grant and Expenditure Decisions*

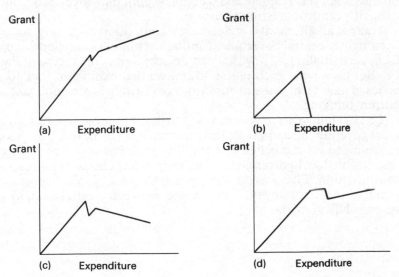

The effects of the grant system on different types of authority – (a) has a low rateable value and a target below its needs assessment, (b) has a very high rateable value, (c) has a comparatively large rateable value,

and (d) has a lower rateable value, but a target above its needs assessment. (We are indebted to Tony Travers for help in preparing these diagrams.)

Change led on to change not merely because the government sought control through influence, but because over-hasty action created its own instability. Targets and penalties had been spatchcocked into a block grant system designed to adjust grant in relation not to targets but to grant-related expenditure. The result was that the relationship between grant and expenditure became in 1981/2 almost random in effect as Figure 6.1 shows. Such a system could not last. For 1983/4 the targets for local government expenditure became more dominant and the penalties more severe. Indeed the frightening course upon which the government is set is prescribed by the internal dynamics of setting penalties based on arbitrary past targets.

Each year penalties are likely to become even more severe, for penalties paid in the previous year are already covered by the existing rate level. Each year the government as it seeks to control through influence will add to penalties. The two dangerous trends are the instability of continuing change and the threat of even steeper penalties pushing influence nearer to becoming direct control. The process is not yet complete and will not be until influence has become explicitly central government control.

There is an alternative, indeed a stark alternative – to rely not on even tighter central government influence but on local control and local accountability. How that can be achieved is the theme of Part IV. But before we reach our solution, we first explore in Part III a series of issues where the assumptions of centralism are dominant in current thinking.

The last four years have come near to destroying our institutions of local government, and yet stability has not been achieved. This book is grounded on the belief that stability is possible on the basis of responsible local government. The only other choice is increasing centralisation. That was the issue posed by the Layfield Report and remains the issue today. The choice between central and local responsibility remains.

Part III

Issues Raised by the Crisis

7 The Treasury and Local Government

An amazing speech about local government was delivered in July 1982 to the Society of Local Authority Chief Executives. It was an address by Mr Leon Brittan, Chief Secretary to the Treasury[1], which provided an insight into Treasury thinking and the attitude adopted by the Conservative government to local government since 1979. He attacked local government for overspending, which was alleged to be damaging the health of the national economy. He asserted that local government, by refusing to stick to central government's targets for expenditure, had broken a constitutional convention and that, if it did not conform in the future and accept the central government's right to give effective guidance, the question would have to be asked 'is the conventional wisdom still right in assuming that local autonomy over priorities and administration of services necessarily implies complete freedom ultimately to determine levels of expenditure by setting the level of rates without any limitation whatsoever?'[2] He was, thus, threatening an effective end to local government, since our system of local government has been based on the right and the duty of a local authority to decide on the level of its expenditure, if financed from its own local tax, the rates – a decision for which it is accountable to its own local electorate.

In Mr Brittan's eyes, and in the view of the Treasury, as is shown in recent books on the Treasury by Mr Joel Barnett (1982, pp. 74–9) and Sir Leo Pliatzky (1982, pp. 117–18, 189–90), local government expenditure, even though financed by rates, is no different from departmental expenditure and should be determined by ministers in central government. Anybody arguing to the contrary is treated as irresponsible or frivolous. Mr Brittan claims that nobody 'seriously' challenges his propositions. However, an increasing number of academics, economists, accountants and officials in local government do argue that[3.] It is significant that the Treasury has never responded directly to this growing body of arguments but goes on repeating its assertions.

We have never argued, as Mr Brittan tried to suggest his opponents argued, that the central government should 'concede total autonomy to local authorities' nor have we said that the central government should 'simply adopt an attitude of casual

insouciance to local government's financial decisions'.[4] Mr
Brittan, other ministers, and even some people from local
government, claim that the central government has 'a concern'
for local government expenditure, or a 'legitimate interest' in it,
because it is such a large component of public expenditure.[5]
However, the problem is to operationalise this 'concern' and
'interest'. In the past the government's concern was expressed by
its forecasts and attempts to influence the aggregate figure of local
government expenditure. But since 1979 it has been expressed by
the claim of the centre 'to set effective targets', to 'set out in
published plans total public spending, including local authority
spending', 'to fix a total for local authority spending'[6] and to
determine such targets not only for local government generally
but for individual local authorities.

We do not deny the right of the central government to have 'a
concern for' or 'an interest in' total local government spending, or
its right to influence that total by exhortation, direct control over
local authority borrowing and by determining the grant it gives to
local government, since grant is the central government's own
expenditure financed by the national taxpayer. But we do
challenge the right of the centre to seek to reach a pre-determined
total by setting binding targets for the expenditure of individual
local authorities, even when financed by rates. Acceptance of the
concern of central government with local government finance
should not become a justification for every intervention. Its
legitimate concern would be better expressed by legislation to
provide a system that encourages proper local accountability.

The central government rightly has the responsibility to
manage the national economy – macro-economic management –
which, Mr Brittan says, is 'based constitutionally on the
sovereignty of Parliament'.[7] But although Parliament is sovereign,
that does not mean that a government department is sovereign.
Ministers and civil servants too often try to pull off a
sleight-of-hand by equating parliamentary sovereignty with departmental supremacy. However, a department can only do what it is
legally empowered to do through powers conferred on its minister by
Parliament, and by the royal prerogative. Parliament has not granted,
even to the Treasury, the power to decide about all expenditure and
all taxes. A government department, like a local authority, is
dependent on Parliament for its authority. Both are co-equal under
Parliament, which has deliberately established local authorities to
provide certain services freer from parliamentary scrutiny,
ministerial direction and civil service control than departments.
Parliament has given to local authorities their own independent
source of taxation with which to finance their own expenditure

decisions. It is not just the central government that has its macro-economic role based on the 'sovereignty of Parliament', local government's autonomy too, and its right to levy its own taxation, are also based on 'the sovereignty of Parliament'.

Mr Brittan argues, as does Mr Tom King, that local authorities have broken the constitutional convention, or 'the old implicit consensus', that 'they accepted the right of central government to fix a total for local authority spending and the informal obligations to adhere to that total'.[8] Local authorities are accused of showing themselves 'less and less willing to accept that central government rightly and legitimately has the power to set effective targets for expenditure'.[9] In fact the government since 1979 has invented this so-called constitutional convention or 'implicit consensus'. In the first years of the public expenditure survey process, in the 1960s and early 1970s, the government made forecasts about local government expenditure in its published annual white papers. But such figures were provisional – they were admitted and accepted as tentative forecasts, dependent on the outcome of the negotiations over rate support grant and on the actual decisions of hundreds of local authorities. During the mid-1970s, following the quadrupling of oil prices, the Labour government sought to cut public expenditure, including local government expenditure, and announced that the 'party was over'. But it sought to achieve its objective by consultation and co-operation with local government, and by seeking to persuade and influence local authorities to conform to the overall targets. It is significant that the Labour government's concern was with total local government expenditure: its measures were designed to influence the aggregate. The major constitutional change has been introduced by the Conservative government, which began to treat the figures for public expenditure, including local government expenditure, not as forecasts nor as aggregates to which local authorities should be influenced, but as firm control figures or pre-determined targets. The mode of action of the centre was no longer to influence the total but to control the particular. Central government, not local government, has broken past conventions; and the conflicts and tensions that now mark central–local relations were created by that action.

Mr Brittan also alleges that local government has been guilty of 'persistent overspending', to such an extent that 'it is immensely damaging to our economic development for one element of government, local government, regularly to distort the position'. This over-spending 'jeopardizes the whole balance which the government and only the government must determine between spending, borrowing and taxation'.[10] He creates the impression of profligate local authorities unsettling the Treasury's fine-tuning of the British economy. However, up to 1980–1 local government expenditure in aggregate regularly came close to the forecasts, deviating by 1 per cent or 2 per cent and most often as under-spending. Since 1980–1 the deviation has been about 5 per cent. The recent suggestion of 7·9 per cent over-spending on central government plans in 1982/3 is in part cash over-spending caused by the unreality of the government's cash limits and represents less than 5 per cent in volume terms. These plans were unrealistic, imposing harsher cuts than the centre imposed on its own departmental expenditure.[11] It regularly cut local government expenditure much deeper than its own. In any case, the accusation of 'overspending' cannot be sustained. Since 1974/5 local government expenditure as a proportion of the gross national product has fallen from 16 per cent to 14 per cent in 1980/1, and as a proportion of total public expenditure from 32 per cent to 28 per cent (and to 25 per cent in 1981/2 on White Paper estimated outcome) while central government expenditure as a proportion of the gross national product has risen from 33 per cent to 35 per cent and as a proportion of total expenditure from 68 per cent to 72 per cent (and to 75 per cent in 1982/3 on the same estimates).[12] Central government has shown less restraint in its own expenditure than has local government, and that trend is clear even with unemployment benefits excluded from the calculation.

Mr Brittan suggests that 'local authorities are unable to manage their budgets',[13] but the reality is that the central government seems unable to control effectively its own expenditure, and seems to erect as a smokescreen or as a diversionary tactic the accusation that others are over-spending and should be more strictly controlled, such as universities, public corporations and, above all, local authorities. It is significant that by July 1982 the only element of public expenditure for which the central government felt able to fix targets for 1983–4 was local government.[14] It was unable to announce targets for its own departmental spending. Control over public expenditure would be much more effective if the central government would concentrate its energies on controlling the expenditure for which it is clearly responsible – its own departmental expenditure – and not distract attention from its responsibilities by unjustified allegations against local authorities.

We deplore Mr Brittan's singling out of local government as the villain of the piece. Its expenditure is only one component of total public expenditure, and far from the largest. The scale of its so-called overspending is not likely to be economically significant. In 1975 Sir Douglas Wass, Permanent Under Secretary of the Treasury, told a

Select Committee that £1 billion extra spending would have a negligible effect on the economy.[15] If £1 billion was tolerable in 1975, £1½ billion is easily tolerable seven years later. This sum, after all, is only a small percentage of total public expenditure of around £120 billion and of the gross national product of £210 billion, and is well within any margin of forecasting error when £3 billion can be the deviation. It is also hard to see that such a figure could have much of an impact on interest rates and hence on industrial investment, especially when the main influence is clearly that of American interest rates. Thus Mr Brittan has exaggerated the impact of alleged local government over-spending. To threaten a major constitutional upheaval – the destruction of local government – for such a relatively insignificant sum and with such relatively unimportant economic consequences is sheer irresponsibility.

Institutions of government are not easily built up, but they can be only too easily destroyed. To attack and threaten local authorities is a dangerous act. Institutions of government need stability. The deliberate creation of instability should not be undertaken without serious cause.

The central government's economic objective is to reduce inflation as a necessary step towards economic recovery. To do so with the current emphasis on monetary policy requires it to curb the growth of the public sector borrowing requirement and money supply. The centre controls local government capital expenditure. Local authorities have to balance their budgets and cannot engage in deficit financing of current expenditure. During 1982–3 local authorities, far from borrowing excessively, have made greater repayments of interest and capital, and have been accused by ministers of under-spending on the capital side. Only the centre can print money and increase the money supply. So local government cannot be blamed. We agree with Mr Brittan that the centre has 'to take account of what local authorities do'[16] – the centre must control borrowing.

We also agree with him in his concern 'about the level of grant which we, as custodians of the taxpayer's interests, make over to local authorities in one form or another'.[17] But that does not justify the attempts to control local authority expenditure financed from the rates. Since 1976/7 the central government's contribution to local authority expenditure through the rate support grant system has been cash limited, so it rightly has grant firmly under its control.

Mr Brittan refers to an argument, recently deployed in the government's Green Paper *Alternatives to Domestic Rates* (Secretaries of State for the Environment, for Scotland and for Wales, 1981) as an objection to the granting to local government of new sources of revenue. It is argued that they would inhibit the freedom of the Chancellor of the Exchequer to devise his fiscal strategy. Mr Brittan said that 'local ratepayers could not spend their money twice. If they are paying it in rates we cannot raise it from them say in income tax'.[18] This argument has little to do with the requirements of macro-economic management. The Chancellor has responsibility for a wide range of taxes over which local government has no control, both direct and indirect, on income, wealth and expenditure. He can use his powers over their rates to counterbalance, if he judges it desirable, the consequences of local government's decisions over its small amount of taxation. To argue that local government's one tax seriously affects the Chancellor's freedom of action has no basis in the reality of the balance of taxation powers. In any case, in other countries local authorities have access to many more taxes whose rates they can vary, and their central finance ministries do not seek to control them all or feel unduly limited in managing their economies, often much more successfully than our own.

Mr Brittan also claimed that central control is necessary over local government expenditure, even if financed by rates, because rate-payers cannot use the money they pay in rates to 'invest it in something more productive. Or use it to buy goods produced somewhere else in the economy'.[19] This argument is a version of the 'crowding-out' thesis, which proclaims that local government expenditure displaces resources from use by the private sector. But that is the point of local accountability; it is about making choices between public and private consumption. If people locally prefer public provision to their own private consumption and are prepared to pay for it out of their local taxes, then they should be allowed to do so; otherwise there is no point in having a system of local government. It should not be for central government to restrict such local choice.

Mr Brittan included a paragraph in his speech which so qualified his argument that it undermined it. 'This is not to say there is an equivalent trade-off between rates and central government taxation. Or that local rates will crowd out private sector spending one for one. But we cannot afford to neglect those relationships. We must take account of them in devising macro-economic policy.'[20] However, 'cannot afford to neglect' and 'take account of' do not justify the centre seeking to control to some pre-determined target local government expenditure financed out of rates. Underlying these phrases are assumptions about the power of central government to control the economy and about the infallibility of its policies that fit uneasily with a stance that recognises the fallibility of government.

Next Mr Brittan mounted a series of arguments that have little to do with central constraint over local government expenditure. It is 'bound also to be interested in how money on services is spent. Many of the services provided by local authorities have to be integrated with

ones which the central government has to offer'.[21] One wonders what
these are, given that British central government has few direct
operational and service-providing functions. The example he gives is
to ensure that local authorities 'are caring for patients which the
Health Service is not'.[22] This point may be relevant for an argument
about the policies of the spending departments but has nothing to do
with Treasury control and constraint over local government
expenditure. In any case, the government's cuts have been heavier on
local government's social services than on the National Health
Service, thus inhibiting local government from providing the
community care needed by patients the health service neglects or
cannot cater for.[23] Mr Brittan also justified central 'interest' in local
expenditure with the sentence, 'And the central government
exercises a degree of responsibility for consistency and standards
across the country'[24] – a very suspect basis on which to justify central
control over local government expenditure financed from rates. A
'degree of responsibility' is too vague, and one has never been
conscious of a Treasury concern for 'consistency and standards' of
services. That is usually the responsibility of the spending departments which must find the present Treasury approach a hindrance to
their attempts to maintain or raise standards or to encourage
consistency. Indeed the evidence from education is that in as far as
there is a growing tendency for standards to vary and in some
authorities to fall below acceptable levels, government targets
requiring reductions on already low standards make matters worse.
Moreover, Mr Brittan apparently justifies intervention in policies, in
standards and in expenditure levels over and above what has been
determined or required by Parliament.

Mr Brittan then switches back to a macro-economic point: 'we are
concerned to ensure that our policies designed to improve the health
of the national economy are not frustrated by the actions of local
authorities. This necessarily means that we are concerned to
influence their decisions about spending and the level of rates . . .
Local authorities are part of government as a whole. And their
actions, like those of the rest of the public sector, can at their worst
stifle enterprise, choke off growth and destroy jobs.'[25] Then we hear
about the impact of high rates on industry and commerce, and how
local government's expenditure and high non-domestic rates are
negating the benefits to industry's profits from cuts in national
taxation. 'Clearly no government concerned to strengthen Britain's
economy and reduce unemployment could stand idly by while that
happened.'[26]

We advocate on page 98 that since non-domestic rates are not an
appropriate tax for local government, because they do not bear
directly on local voters, they should be transformed into a national

tax. In this way the Treasury could have full control over all taxes on industry and commerce, without the difficulties involved in trying to control local government expenditure and rate levels. In any case, the impact of rates on industry is exaggerated. They form only a very small part of costs and are comparable to bills for heating, lighting and the telephone. The recent difficulties of business have arisen less from rates and more from the recession and lack of demand, from high interest payments and the national government's national insurance contributions and surcharge. Mr Brittan's points may reinforce the central government's right to be 'concerned' and to take an 'interest' in local government expenditure, but not to try to control it, and rates, through pre-set targets.

Mr Brittan has merely made repeated assertions about the need for the centre to control local government expenditure. He produces no sustained argument or answer to those who argue that for macro-economic objectives he need rely on control over local government borrowing and over grant, and on central government persuasion, exhortation and influence.[27] There is no economic justification for the centre to control local government expenditure, even if it is about a quarter of total public expenditure, as long as it is financed from taxes that bear on local voters. Indeed Mr Brittan could best achieve the Treasury's macro-economic goals by making local government its ally in the battle for the wise use of resources. If local authorities financed more of their expenditure from their own local revenue, a better balance of spending and taxing would be attained. Instead of seeking ever more central control, which only serves to turn local authorities into pressure groups asking for more, Mr Brittan should campaign for local authorities to be less dependent on grant, to give up the non-domestic rate and to obtain the lion's share of their revenue from domestic rates and local income tax. With these reforms local authorities would behave more responsibly, since if they wanted to spend more, they would have to increase taxes on their local voters. 'Concern' would be expressed by putting local government finance on a basis that strengthens local accountability.

It is ironical that a minister from the Conservative Party, which many have seen as the champion of local decision-making against centralised bureaucracy, should have made one of the most fierce attacks on local government, threatening it in effect with abolition. His menacing message was: 'Local government spending plays such an important part in our economy that a failure to overcome the problem of overspending is bound to lead ultimately to developments which the friends of local government will find extremely unwelcome. It is bound to cause central government to intervene ever more obtrusively and seek ever greater powers over local authority finances.'[28] We have been warned. But the justification for such an increase in central intervention is based on a defective economic diagnosis, erroneous history, a faulty perspective on local government expenditure and rating, and a failure to recognise that the measures proposed exacerbate the problems they are trying to cure. The only merit in Mr Brittan's speech is that he, the Treasury and the government have revealed themselves clearly as overt centralisers who see local government simply as a branch of central government.

Postscript

The Treasury returned to its offensive against local government in September 1982 with a speech by Mr Jock Bruce-Gardyne, Economic Secretary to the Treasury, to a conference of the Chartered Institute of Public Finance and Accountancy.[29] He deployed many of the arguments used by Mr Brittan. He observed that since about 'half of what local authorities spend comes straight from central government. No one can deny that we have an interest in that.' He expressed anxiety that 'the more local authorities take in rates, the less the central government can take in other taxes'. He asserted that local government expenditure and taxation will 'to a greater or lesser extent' displace other spending elsewhere – the crowding-out thesis. He claimed the central government could not afford 'to be wholly indifferent to the impact of local taxation upon the corporate ratepayer'. He claimed that the government 'has a responsibility for' the consistency of some service standards, for example education, and 'to ensure that the resources going into education, in aggregate, bear a reasonable relationship to the resources being invested in, say, health or defence. The central government therefore has to take an interest in the pattern of local authority services as well as in their total cost.' He went on, 'Whether you look at where the money comes from, therefore, or what it goes [on], we in central government are bound to take a view about the aggregate of local authority spending, about its distribution between services, about its incidence between regions, and about its effects on the income distribution'. However, taking a view on, and having an interest in, such broad aggregates, does not justify detailed intervention into individual local authorities, and their particular spending and rating decisions.

He argued that local government spending 'in excess of the levels which we have indicated will be a disruptive influence in the economy', which will delay 'an early return to sound growth'. He concluded that 'as long as local government can backstop its own spending plans with its own power to tax the wealth of the country, and as long as the sums involved are so vast, we must look to local government to abide by the guidelines for conduct with which they are informed'. This view, he said, was 'a restatement of the concordat which has traditionally governed our relationships'.

He did not threaten local government as explicitly as had Mr Brittan. He said, 'We are not opposed in principle to the existing degree of financial independence for local authorities when it is coupled with responsible management and electoral accountability'. It is a pity that in practice the government has undermined their financial independence, so disrupted the financial framework as to make responsible management impossible and has shown no interest in encouraging their electoral accountability.

He made some fascinating remarks about local government borrowing. We agree with his view that 'local authority borrowing, however it is financed, will feed through to higher monetary growth and higher inflationary pressure' – which is why we support firm central government control over local government borrowing, although strict devotees of the market should be prepared to let local authorities borrow subject only to the market discipline of interest rates. He expressed worry that the government was unable to forecast local authority borrowing accurately in the short-term, even blaming local authority treasurers for having 'so little control of their borrowing'. But the government would be better advised to ensure that it has effective policy instruments to control local borrowing, given its critical role in the management of the economy, rather than concentrating its efforts on trying to pre-determine the current expenditure of local authorities, even if financed from local rates.

Notes to Chapter 7

1   H.M. Treasury, Press Statement, text of a speech by Rt Hon Leon Brittan, QC, MP, Chief Secretary to the Treasury, to the Society of Local Authority Chief Executives (SOLACE) at the Viking Hotel in York on Friday 16 July 1982.
2   Brittan speech, p. 11.
3   e.g. House of Commons, Second Report from the Environment Committee, *Enquiry into Methods of Financing Local Government in the Context of the Government's Green Paper (Cmnd 8449)*, Appendices, Volume III, 27 July 1982, HC (1981–2) 217–III, pp. 12–25. Also Richard Jackman, 'Does central government need to control the total of local government spending?', *Local Government Studies*, May–June 1982, pp. 75–90.
4   Brittan speech, pp. 7 and 8.
5   For example, a speech by Mr Tom King, Minister of State at the Department of the Environment, to the conference of the Chartered Institute of Public Finance and Accountancy at Harrogate, 4 June 1982, Department of the Environment, Press Notice No. 196. 'The Minister said that the vast majority of people recognise that the central government has a legitimate interest in the total level of local government spending.' (p. 1). Also in his evidence before the Environment

Committee, HC (1981–2), 217–II, Vol. II, p. 247. Also see the views of the Society of County Treasurers, *County Councils Gazette*, October 1981, p. 202.
6   Brittan speech, pp. 8 and 9.
7   Brittan speech, p. 10.
8   Brittan speech, p. 8.
9   Brittan speech, p. 9.
10   *ibid.*
11   See pages 62–71 below.
12   Central Statistical Office (CSO), *Economic Trends*; CSO, *Financial Statistics*; Chartered Institute of Public Finance and Accountancy (CIPFA), *Local Government Trends*; White Papers on Public Expenditure. All annual series.
13   Brittan speech, p. 9.
14   Speech by Mr Michael Heseltine in the House of Commons, HC Debs (1981–2), 27 July 1982, Cols 923–31.
15   House of Commons, Fourteenth Report from the Expenditure Committee, *The Motor Vehicle Industry*, Vol. II, HC (1974–5) 617–II, pp. 201–2.
16   Brittan speech, p. 7.
17   *ibid.*
18   *ibid.*
19   *ibid.*
20   *ibid.*
21   *ibid.*
22   *ibid.*
23   See pages 62–71 below.
24   Brittan speech, p. 7.
25   Brittan speech, pp. 7–8.
26   Brittan speech, p. 8.
27   Enoch Powell has written, 'By all means limit Exchequer grants and Government loans: but every monetarist knows that rates cannot cause inflation and councils cannot print money. So why set every elected council by the ears from one end of Britain to the other? It doesn't add up.' *Sunday Express*, 11 October 1981.
28   Brittan speech, p. 9.
29   H.M. Treasury, Press Statement, text of a speech by Jock Bruce-Gardyne MP, Economic Secretary to the Treasury, to the annual regional seminar of the Chartered Institute of Public Finance and Accountancy in Torquay on 30 September 1982. The relevant sections are pp. 7–11.

8 The White Paper on Public Expenditure and the Targets

The White Paper on Public Expenditure

The annual White Paper on Public Expenditure, titled *The Government's Expenditure Plans*, symbolises the confusion in responsibility that underlies the continuing crisis in central–local relations. The White Paper is the culmination of the process of resource allocation in central government, which determines the level of total expenditure and its distribution between the various activities of central government. To that extent it is a process familiar enough to local government. It is the normal function of budgeting, which any organisation has to undertake in determining its level and distribution of expenditure.

The confusing feature of the process that results in the White Paper is that it includes local government expenditure (for which central government is not directly responsible) in exactly the same way and in the same form as central government's own expenditure, even though that local government expenditure is not financed by central government but by the rates.

It has been accepted for too long that the White Paper should treat local government expenditure in this way. It is regarded as natural even by many in local government. Yet it is far from clear that this arrangement is sensible or desirable. The inclusion of local government's expenditure in the process of resource allocation within central government and in its statement of its plans for public expenditure is a source of confusion over responsibility for local government expenditure. By treating local government expenditure in just the same way as central government expenditure, the White Paper implies that local government expenditure is under the direct responsibility of central government. Yet individual local authorities make the critical decisions on this expenditure and on the levels of rates required to finance that expenditure.

The treatment of local government expenditure in the White Paper also distorts the budgetary process of central government. In drawing up their estimates of expenditure, ministers whose departments are concerned with local government face a choice of grappling with expenditure which is their own direct responsibility, and on which they make the real decision, or expenditure which is the direct responsibility of local government and on which the real decisions will be made by local authorities.

The Social Services Secretary has to make choices between expenditure on health on which his or her decision actually determines the amount of resources received by health authorities, and expenditure on social services where the final decisions are actually made by local authorities. Inevitably the Secretary of State has imposed cuts on the targets for local authorities, as Table 8.1 shows.

Table 8.1   *Health and Social Services Current Expenditure*

Health and social services current expenditure	1978/9 (actual)	1981/2	Change	% change
	(£m. at 1980 survey prices)			
National health services (National Health Service)	7,217	7,488	+ 271	+ 3·8
Personal social services (local authority services)	1,256	1,192	– 64	– 5·1

Source: Chancellor of the Exchequer, *The Government's Expenditure Plans 1981-82 to 1983–84*, 1981, Cmnd 8175.

He in effect chooses between setting real totals for his own departmental activities which will actually determine expenditure and fictitious totals for local government's activities which will not necessarily determine expenditure. Faced with Treasury pressure for cuts in expenditure he can cut the national expenditure total, knowing that 'irresponsible local authorities' need not implement the cuts, and maintain or even increase his department's expenditure. Thus the Social Services Secretary has tended to concentrate cuts on local authority social services while preserving or increasing health services expenditure, despite the fact that the policy has been to move patients out of long-term institutional care, whose expenditure falls on the health service, to community care whose costs fall on local government's social services. This result follows directly from a resource allocation process that allows ministers to fix totals both for expenditure which is subject to their control and for expenditure which is subject to local authority control. They have the opportunity to choose between real departmental cuts and illusory notional cuts.

Other factors increase the bias. A minister is not likely to acknowledge that there is waste in his own department. He will not, therefore, put forward proposals to reduce expenditure by eliminating waste in his own department, although it is commonplace for ministers to justify cuts in the expenditure figures for local authorities as a stimulus for the elimination of waste. In the final resort a minister will fight for his own department's expenditure, while he sees no need to fight for local authorities' expenditure.

Because the figures for expenditure once totalled become the targets for local government expenditure to which central government has recently begun to demand adherence, it is important for local government to expose this process. The targets are determined in a way which inevitably leads to more severe targets being set for local government expenditure than for central government expenditure. In recent years local government has sought greater involvement in the process leading to the White Paper on Public Expenditure. That quest has been a mistake. The White Paper remains in the end a cabinet and central government decision. The confusion of responsibility and the bias in the process would still remain, even with greater local government participation.

The demand that local government should make is for the removal of local government expenditure from the White Paper on Public Expenditure. That step would both clarify responsibility and make more meaningful the process of resource allocation underlying the White Paper. Both results are in the interests of good government.

The Targets for 1981/2

The consequences of the bias in the process are found in the details of the targets set. The government's target for local government revenue expenditure in 1981/2 represents a 5·6 per cent reduction in volume compared with 1978/9. It is widely believed in local government that this represents an unfair reduction in local government expenditure when compared with a reduction required of central government itself.

The White Paper on Public Expenditure shows that such a belief is much too favourable to the government. The reality is that, however it is measured, while government requires substantial cuts in local government expenditure, it does not require it in its own. If the current crisis has one clear cause it is that the government is asking of local government reductions in expenditure which are unreasonable by the criteria it applies to itself.

The comparison in Table 8.2 includes capital expenditure, and one can also compare current expenditure (Table 8.3). It is often argued that this merely reflects the inevitable growth in social security in a period of growing unemployment. However, if the social security programme is excluded the position is as shown in Table 8.4. On each basis central government expenditure is planned to increase by over 4 per cent, while local government expenditure is planned to decrease by at least 4·7 per cent.

There is a case to be answered that central government has attempted to impose severe cuts on local government that it has not imposed on itself. Ministers faced with a choice between cutting central government expenditures for which they are directly responsible and local government expenditures for which they are not directly responsible can too easily take the option of cutting local government expenditure, knowing that local councillors will have to bear the unpopularity.

Table 8.2 *Total Expenditure (Capital and Current) from Table 1.10 (Excluding Debt Interest and Other Adjustment)*

	1978/9	1981/2	Change	% change
	(£m.)			
Central government	54,737	58,655	+ 3,918	+ 7·2
Local government	21,426	19,200	− 2,226	− 10·4

Table 8.3 *Total Expenditure (Current) from Table 1.10*

Central government	49,732	53,572	+ 3,840	+ 7·7
Local government	16,911	16,112	− 799	− 4·7

Table 8.4 *Total Current Expenditure (from Tables 1.10 and 2.12) (Excluding the Social Security Programme)*

Central government	31,088	32,411	+ 1,323	+ 4·3
Local government	16,911	16,112	− 799	− 4·7

Source: Cmnd 8175.

Lest it be thought that these arguments are exaggerated, Table 8.5 shows the position, programme by programme. Whereas in every category of local government expenditure except law and order central government sought a decrease, it planned a decrease in only two of the ten categories into which its own expenditure was divided, and in only one category was that as great as the decreases planned in local government expenditure. It is significant that that category was housing where the cuts were largely in subsidies to local government. It was a cut in local government expenditure in another way. However, it can be said that in no category of central government expenditure was any significant cut imposed, whereas in five out of seven categories in local government expenditure outside Northern Ireland a cut of over 7 per cent was imposed.

Table 8.5   *Total Expenditure (Capital and Current) by Programme*

	1978/9	1981/2	Change	% change
	(£m. at 1980 prices)			
Central government				
Defence and overseas services	11,026	11,324	+ 298	+ 2·7
Agriculture, food, fish and forestry	791	812	+ 21	+ 2·7
Industry, energy, trade and employment	3,435	3,899	+ 464	+ 13·5
Transport	1,202	1,208	+ 6	+ 0·5
Housing	2,216	1,598	− 618	− 27·9
Education and science, arts and libraries	1,496	1,451	− 45	− 3·0
Health and personal social services	7,658	7,970	+ 312	+ 4·1
Social security	18,644	21,161	+ 2,517	+ 13·5
Other programmes including Scotland, Wales and Northern Ireland	7,456	7,834	+ 378	+ 5·1
Government lending to nationalised industry	812	1,400	+ 588	+ 72·4
Local government				
Transport	1,627	1,447	− 180	− 11·1
Housing	2,385	1,348	− 1,037	− 43·5
Other environmental services	2,513	2,219	− 294	− 11·7
Law, order and protective services	1,998	2,181	+ 183	+ 9·2
Education and sciences, arts and libraries	7,675	7,093	− 582	− 7·6
Personal social services	1,315	1,264	− 51	− 3·9
Other programmes (Great Britain)	3,564	3,304	− 260	− 7·3
Local authorities in Northern Ireland	349	346	− 3	− 0·9

Source: Cmnd 8175, Table 1.9.

It will be argued that it is merely that the services of central government represent national priorities and that in no sense have different criteria been applied to local government expenditure. The only way that this issue can be tested is by comparing similar or related functions carried out by central and local government and testing whether the targets for local government expenditure are the same or more severe than those for central government expenditure. This can be carried out only for certain activities, but it does provide a real test of whether central government is setting reasonable targets for local government expenditure.

Table 8.6 *Arts and Libraries, Current Expenditure (from Table 2.10)*

	1978/9	1981/2	Change	% change
	(£m. at 1980 survey prices)			
Central government	128	139	+ 11	+ 8·6
Local authorities	234	199	– 35	– 15·0

Table 8.7 *Road Maintenance, Current Expenditure (from Table 2.6)*

Department of Transport	104	118	+ 14	+ 13·5
Local authorities	593	517	– 76	– 12·8

Table 8.8 *Transport Administration, Current Expenditure (from Table 2.6)*

Roads and transport administration (Department of Transport)	27	28	+ 1	+ 3·7
Roads and transport administration by local authorities	176	155	– 21	– 11·9

Table 8.9 *Housing Administration, Current Expenditure (from Table 2.7)*

Central government	18	21*	+ 3	+ 16·7
Local government	85	70*	– 15	– 17·6

* 1980/81 figures (1981/82 are not available).

Table 8.10 *Health and Social Services, Current Expenditure (from Table 2.11)*

National health services	7,217	7,488	+ 271	+ 3·8
Personal social services (local authority)	1,256	1,192	– 64	– 5·1

Table 8.6 shows expenditure on arts and libraries. It is difficult to see any justification, if the same criteria were being applied, why central government expenditure should increase when local govern-

ment is asked to cut the same expenditure by 15 per cent. As Table 8.7 shows, the scale of increase proposed in central government expenditure on highways maintenance is excessive in comparison to the scale of decrease in local government expenditure. A cut in administration at local level could be argued to be in accordance with central government policy, but it is then difficult to understand why there is no equivalent reduction planned at central government level (Table 8.8). Similarly, in housing administration (Table 8.9) it is hard to see how central government can justify such a striking difference in their plans for expenditure on central government administration when compared with local government administration. Finally, Table 8.10 shows spending on health and social services on which we have commented above.

In all the fields in which it has been possible to make comparisons, central government has set targets for local government which involve severe cuts while setting targets for themselves that, far from involving cuts, actually involve increases even in fields like administration which the government is committed to cut. There is strong evidence that the cuts being demanded are unreasonable by the criteria central government has established for itself. If that is correct, then it is hard to see how central government can justify the penalties it imposes or the threats it is making. The crisis is of its own making. It has imposed targets on local government that it has not imposed on itself.

The Targets Set for 1982/3

The bias in the process had the same result in targets for 1982/3. These new targets are set in cash terms, rather than (as previously) in real terms. This change can make interpretation more difficult. One conclusion can, however, be drawn. Yet again the targets set for local government expenditure are more severe than for central government itself.

The tables both confirm and illustrate this conclusion. The tables each show the planned change in expenditure from 1980–1 – the last year for which actual expenditure figures are available – to 1982–3. Most tables show increases in expenditure, for the very simple reason that the expenditure is set out in cash terms. Table 8.11 shows that, whereas total central government expenditure over the two years is planned to increase by 24·3 per cent, probably representing a real increase in expenditure, local government expenditure is planned to increase by less than half that figure, representing a substantial real decrease in expenditure – on the assumption that inflation will be running at 20–22 per cent over the two-year period.

Table 8.11   *Total Expenditure (Capital and Current) from Table 1.11 (Excluding Debt Interest and Other Adjustment)*

	1980/1	1982/3	Change	% change
	(£m. cash)			
Central government	67,701	84,127	+ 16,426	+ 24·3
Local government	25,109	28,036	+ 2,927	+ 11·7

Table 8.12   *Total Expenditure (Current from Table 1.12)*

Central government	61,632	78,199	+ 16,567	+ 26·9
Local government	20,678	23,750	+ 3,072	+ 14·9

Table 8.13   *Total Current Expenditure (from Table 1.12 and 2.12) (Excluding the Social Security Programme)*

Central government	38,192	46,169	+ 7,977	+ 20·9
Local government	20,678	23,750	+ 3,072	+ 14·9

Table 8.14   *A Arts and Libraries, Current Expenditure (from Table 2.10)*

Central government	175	205	+ 30	+ 17·1
Local government	278	302	+ 24	+ 8·6

Table 8.15   *B Road Maintenance, Current Expenditure (from Table 2.6)*

Department of Transport	117	166	+ 49	+ 41·9
Local authorities	665	787	+ 122	+ 18·3

Table 8.16   *C Transport Administration, Current Expenditure (from Table 2.6)*

Roads and transport administration (DTp)	34	38	+ 4	+ 11·8
Roads and transport administration by local authorities	226	170	− 56	− 24·8

Table 8.17   *D Housing Administration, Current Expenditure (from Table 2.7)*

Central government	22	30*	+ 8	+ 36·4
Local government	118	92*	− 26	− 22·0

Table 8.18   *E   Health and Social Services, Current Expenditure (from Table 2.11)*

| National health services | 9,110 | 10,986 | + 1,876 | + 20·6 |
| Personal social services | 1,618 | 1,857 | + 239 | + 14·8 |

* 1981/82 figures (1982/83 are not available).

It will then be said that an increase in central government expenditure is inevitable, given an increase in unemployment and in the social security programme generally. But Table 8.13 shows that, even when this programme is left out of the central government expenditure figure, central government expenditure is planned to increase substantially more in cash terms than local government expenditure, where a substantial reduction in real terms is planned by central government.

This conclusion is no accident. It is almost inevitable, given the process by which these targets are arrived at, that they will be set on a more severe basis for local government than for central government. It would be difficult, indeed, to design a stranger system of resource allocation by which ministers can evade the Treasury's policy of expenditure cuts by cutting expenditure for which they are not responsible, and which is not their own expenditure.

If anybody doubts the reality of this analysis, let them look at the choices made by ministers in those activities in which both central government and local governments are directly engaged.

- Table 8.14 shows that while central government's expenditure on the arts and libraries is to increase by 17·1 per cent in cash terms, an increase of only 8·6 per cent in cash terms is planned for local government expenditure, representing a severe and savage cut. No reason is given for this very striking difference.
- Table 8.15 shows that while a 41·9 per cent increase is planned for central government's expenditure on road maintenance, representing a very substantive real increase, for local government only a 18·3 per cent increase in cash terms is planned, representing a probable reduction in real terms.
- For transport administration central government is planning to increase its expenditure in cash terms by 11·8 per cent, while local government expenditure in cash terms is expected to fall by the incredible figure of 24·8 per cent in cash terms (Table 8.16) – representing an even greater reduction in real terms.
- For housing administration no breakdown is given for 1982–3 between central government and local government expenditure but, incredibly, between 1980–1 and 1981–2, while local government expenditure is estimated to fall in cash terms by 22

per cent, central government expenditure is anticipated to rise by 36·4 per cent (Table 8.17).

• Finally, in a period when central government's policy is to move patients from institutional into community care, its target for health service expenditure is very significantly above its target for social services, which involves a very real cut in expenditure (Table 8.18).

There can be no greater condemnation of the whole process by which local government expenditure targets are set than this set of figures. It is almost as if ministers consider they can write down any figure they wish for local government expenditure, as long as it helps to protect their own departmental expenditure. Yet these are the targets by which ministers then proceed to judge local government expenditure. Surely the time is coming when local government should challenge this meaningless process. If local government targets were set not by this strange process, but on the same basis as the targets for central government, there would be no question of local government overspending. By central government's standards for its own expenditure, local government is under-spending.

9 The Allegation Against Over-Spending Local Authorities

The fact that some local authorities are regarded by the Secretary of State as over-spending is not in itself a problem requiring action by the Secretary of State. For the Secretary of State to say that certain authorities are over-spending is merely to state that the views of those authorities on the proper level of expenditure for their areas differ from the views of the Secretary of State. That is not a fact to be regretted. It is not a sign of a conspiracy against the government. Local authorities are constituted to make their own decisions about expenditure levels and not to make the Secretary of State's decisions.

Some local authorities will be spending more and others less than the Secretary of State considers appropriate. They will be judged by that imperfect and varying standard – the opinion of Secretaries of State – both over-spenders and under-spenders. Because the Secretary of State's judgement is expressed in a figure of grant-related expenditure based on a formula, it may appear objective. But the appearance is superficial. The weight given to each factor is a judgement. Grant-related expenditure for each authority merely gives expression to the judgement of the Secretary of State. Change any factor weight and the figure changes. A future Secretary of State might believe in massive subsidisation of public transport, and some of today's over-spenders could well become average or even under-spenders.

It is only when measured by the judgement of the Secretary of State that local authorities are categorised as over-spenders and under-spenders. But it is neither his duty nor his responsibility to make that judgement. The Secretary of State is not elected to make a judgement on the need for expenditure in a particular authority, and previous Secretaries of State have not attempted to categorise authorities as either over-spenders or under-spenders. The local authority on the other hand is elected to make just that judgement. To say that a local authority is over-spending (or indeed under-spending, for the same arguments apply) is merely to record that a local authority carrying out its duty, for which it has been elected, of determining its own expenditure differs from the views of the Secretary of State on the need for expenditure in that locality; but the Secretary of State has not been elected to make that judgement.

This view may be difficult to accept – and yet it has always been accepted until now. Until now, Secretaries of State have not been concerned with what particular authorities were spending. That does not mean that they approved of what those authorities were spending. They did not regard it as their business. That did not mean that past Secretaries of State would have approved of the spending of Lambeth or the Greater London Council, any more than they approved, at the other extreme, of the spending of Oxfordshire or East Sussex. They recognised that it was a matter for those authorities and their electors.

That is where the mistake has been made. Obviously, it is likely that a Conservative government will not like the expenditure policies of a Labour-controlled GLC any more than a Labour government will like the expenditure policies of East Sussex. That is not a reason for legislation. Local authorities' discretion is about discretion to do what central government does not like. Any central government will give local authorities the freedom to do what central government likes; it is the freedom to do otherwise that counts.

In the end, it is for the local electorate to make a judgement on the expenditure policies of the local authority. In Lambeth and the Lothians, they have done so. It is not for the Secretary of State to intervene. By intervening he undermines the importance of local elections, just at a time when the signs are that they are assuming a new importance. He is in effect saying it does not matter what happens in local elections, and that he will intervene to impose a reduction in expenditure. He is substituting himself for the local electorate.

Secretaries of State should be concerned with national choice, and the local authorities and the local electorate with local choice. He may not like the local choice, but it should remain the local choice.

10 Issues for the Education Service

The issues raised in the crisis of central–local government relationships have affected not merely local government generally and local government finance but also the various services provided by local authorities. When the central government complains that local government is over-spending it means that particular local authorities are spending too much on social services, housing, the police, environmental services, and above all on education, which is the service on which local government spends the most. In this chapter we explore some of the issues which the present crisis poses for the education service.

A National or a Local Service

It has always been misleading to describe the English education system in that much repeated phrase 'a national service locally administered'. The reality has been very different. The education system has been founded on a school-based service, over which the local authority and to a less extent central government have operated particular instruments of control and influence.

The danger is that the phrase 'a national service locally administered', although a misleading description, has had wide appeal and has led many to misunderstand how the education system has actually worked. It has conferred an undue importance on the actions of central government as shaping the character of the education system and has denied the very real and probably much greater importance of the school and of the local authority.

It will be argued that the existence, at least until recently, of broad uniformities of educational provision or of accepted minimum standards shows the presence of a national service and hence reflects the significant impact of central government. If one merely means by a national service the existence of those uniformities and standards, then the phrase may be justified, but then the use of the phrase tells nothing about the impact or influence of central government. The uniformities that were established and the standards that were reached were much more the results of shared professional and public aspiration than of central control. They arose from the pressure of professional education officers and teachers within the education service, from the pressure of a variety of interest groups, local as well as national, urging better provision, and from the general pressure of parties, parents and the public. Together they shaped a common view of appropriate and desirable standards, which evolved over time. There were differences in practice and in policies between local authorities, but they were differences set within this common culture, which limited the extent of the differences. This uniformity was not imposed by the central government, but was uniformity to the extent required by the system, and was in fact freely chosen by different education authorities. Indeed, it is better to think of common standards rather than of national standards centrally imposed.

Advance from Diversity and Difference

Local government, which includes the local government of education, represents a diffusion of power in our society. This diffusion promotes diversity and difference within limits set by a shared culture. That diversity has been the source of new initiatives and experimentation and is the basis for the social learning that comes from trying out a variety of policies. Advance in education has been achieved less by central government than by initiatives taken in particular local authorities and particular schools.

Individual local education authorities, or schools within them, developed community colleges, different forms of comprehensive education, experiments in in-service training, and new relationships between parents and schools. From these specific initiatives central government, along with other local education authorities, learnt and then helped transmit the lessons to others. Diversity is not to be regretted in any complex social system, since without such diversity learning is restricted and advance inhibited. In the government of education advance has come from this diversity, based on diffusion of power.

Has acceptable diversity turned into unacceptable disparity? The talk is not now of rich diversity, but rather that differences between local authorities in their levels of expenditure have become unacceptable disparities. We note the views now expressed, but look forward to evidence not merely of the extent of these disparities but their cause.

If disparities have grown, it is no accident that they have grown during the new phase of central government intervention, setting targets for each and every local authority and requiring in 1981–2 for each local authority a reduction of 5·6 per cent in expenditure on its expenditure of three years previously. Unacceptable disparities have been a consequence of increased central government intervention. The government is seeking to over-determine the workings of local authorities. Faced with a problem it itself has created, it moves to further intervention, creating yet more problems.

If there is a crisis in education, it is the result of excessive central government intervention. There is an alternative. Rather than move from intervention to intervention until finally total control is reached, the alternative is to move in the other direction, by creating conditions of real local accountability.

Part IV

A Local Government for the Future

11 False Trails

So far we have described the problems of local government in the crisis of recent years. We believe that the time has now come for a re-structuring of local government on a firm base, so that it will be clearly responsible for major functions and clearly accountable to its own electorate.

Some recognise the problems, but believe there are simple solutions. They consider that the problems of local government finance will be resolved by:

	(i)	the transfer of responsibility for part of local government expenditure to central government;
or	(ii)	the prescription of minimum standards for expenditure;
or	(iii)	the creation of a separate block grant for education.

Others believe that decentralisation must be built on regional rather than local government, or that a greater involvement of MPs is required in supervising the activities of local government.

These alleged solutions will in fact weaken or destroy local government because they are not concerned to strengthen local government responsibility or its accountability at local level. These approaches are false trails, because they do not solve the problems; they evade them, distract attention from better solutions and lead in the wrong direction – to erode local government and increase centralisation.

Transfers of Responsibilities to Central Government

Since many friends of local government are tempted from time to time to advocate this policy it is important to analyse its arguments and their consequences.

The essence of the approach is that one should, first, consider the nature of services. Those which are truly local in character would remain with local government, while those in which the central government is concerned, to secure national standards and control expenditure, would be allocated to central government. Each level would finance its own cluster of services. As a result, some services presently the responsibility of local government would be transferred to the centre, as would their financing, relieving local government of the need to finance these 'national' services.

A variant of this proposition is that instead of transferring the total responsibility for providing a service, the responsibility for the cost of the service, in whole or in part, could be transferred. In any case, it is argued, a financial burden will have been lifted from the ratepayer, while the centre will no longer be interfering in local authorities' provision and spending on their local range of services. But the relief to the ratepayer is illusory. As a consequence of the transfer to the centre of a service or of its cost the centre would incur additional expenditure and would probably reduce its grant to local government, leaving the ratepayer with the same amount to raise. The centre's only alternative would be to raise additional taxation itself – hardly a popular option.

Nor can services be divided simply into local or central. Central and local interests are intertwined and impinge on each other in most of the services of local government. Local government provides the basis for diversity in the provision of services within the uniformities required by society. Any attempt to divide services into local or national services would impose artificial categories into which services had to be fitted, leading to a weakening of local government by passing over to the centre services in which there was a significant local interest.

Dividing a single service into its financing and administration and transferring only the former to the centre is also a recipe for irresponsibility. Such a system provides an incentive to local authorities to maximise budgets and blame the centre for failing to supply enough resources. Local government would become a pressure group channelling claims for higher expenditure to the national government. Such a transfer is in effect a 100 per cent specific grant, which must inevitably lead to detailed scrutiny and control over local provision by the centre, seeking to ensure standards were attained and bids for money justified. It would ultimately lead to greater expenditure as the centre found itself unable to resist the weight of pressures from all local authorities, which converged on the centre, urging more spending. Economy and efficiency would suffer.

Transfer of services, parts of services or of their financing to the centre would also fundamentally damage local government, as the government of its local community. A local authority should be able to consider the total effect on its locality of a wide range of services, to explore the inter-relationships between them and decide on its priorities, and provide that mixture of services most fitting to the needs and wishes of that particular area. Transfers to the centre would diminish the capacity of local government to be genuine community government. Attempts at corporate management and planning of services would be frustrated. The enthusiasm and interest of both councillors and officers would be weakened. Few energetic and able people would want to serve in such a constrained authority. Transfers would damage innovation and initiative in the development of individual services, and their responsiveness to local needs. If the centre were given financial responsibility, it would inevitably seek to impose on local authorities its view of what they should be doing, and to eliminate variation. It would lead inevitably through the requirements of financial control to uniformity, standardisation and limitation on experiment. Artificial national standards would prevail, unresponsive to local conditions, needs and wishes.

Transfer to the centre of only part of a service, say of its financing or salaries of staff, would also mean fragmented responsibility. Local authorities would not be fully in control of the service and its development. Financing of staff, for example teachers' salaries, must inevitably mean control over staffing numbers and gradings. The centre would be involved in staffing issues on an individual basis so that personnel would become in effect central employees. Choices involving changes in staffing and in other costs would be divided between the centre and the local authority. Confusion and ambiguity would reign as central and local government sought to push a service in the direction each thought appropriate.

Finally, transfer of only financial responsibility is unlikely to be the last stage. The implication of such a transfer is that there is little local discretion in the service, and the question is raised as to whether the service itself should remain in local government. The confusion of responsibility already identified would be resolved by a central government takeover.

This topic was fully explored by the Layfield Committee whose report provides a still-relevant conclusion. It argued that transfer would result in a significant loss of the discretion that local authorities now have. It would increase expenditure pressures on the government and departments and lead to divided responsibility. It would not necessarily achieve the purpose for which transfer is advocated, namely either reducing tax burdens or increasing efficiency. It would prevent local authorities from effectively fulfilling their roles in the provision and co-ordination of local services and, in so doing, would fundamentally alter the character of local government.

Minimum Standards

It is also often assumed that central government needs to control local government in order to ensure that national minimum standards are achieved. This assertion requires rebuttal. National minimum standards, in statutes or statutory instruments, are in fact rare. Most mandatory obligations laid on local authorities are general, empowering local authorities to perform certain functions, giving them duties and laying down procedures, while leaving local authorities discretion about the level and extent of the service provided, its frequency and intensity. The standards which have emerged are not nationally determined and imposed minimum standards but common standards that have evolved, and continually develop, from a complex mixture of pressures, including accumulated past practices of local authorities, professional views, political influences, and the urging of pressure groups both local and national. Such standards are in effect standards achieved through local choice.

National minimum standards are inevitably 'input' standards, such as staff ratios, unit costs and physical measurements of buildings and sites. They concentrate on what can be nationally quantified. They do not indicate if management is effective, efficient or extravagant, and are in effect requirements to spend irrespective of what is achieved. They are not standards of performance, the only relevant standards. The way to achieve such 'output' standards is not by national prescription, but to allow local authorities to experiment.

National minimum standards will inevitably be crude, a result of averaging out to the lowest common denominator. They can never take account of the varied characteristics of different local authorities, such as their physical features, social composition, resources and needs. If they are specified in detail, then an increase in central civil servants will be needed to draw up standards that can be operationalised in each locality. National minimum standards will be rigid, unable to take account of local conditions or to respond flexibly and quickly to changing circumstances, in the environment, in technology, in views and values.

National minimum standards once set cannot remain stable. Government will come under constant pressure from various sources to raise the standards, from professional bodies, pressure groups, parties, MPs, ministers and civil servants, all eager to improve and expand services. Thus the centre will become inundated, and pushed to intervene. If the central government is held responsible for standards a vast increase in centralisation will occur as society's pressures converge on it to raise the standards.

National minimum standards inevitably based on input measures inhibit experiment and hinder creative thought about policy. Within a context of national minimum standards a local authority would not have to ponder deeply about a problem. It would simply meet the minimum standard. It would not have to explore the consequences, side effects, political and social implications and impact on the locality.

High common standards are most likely to be uncovered and

encouraged by the free play of local authority experiment and pioneering to find the policy solutions most appropriate to their local areas and problems. It is nonsense to argue that if the centre failed to lay down minimum standards then some local authorities would allow their services to deteriorate and citizens would be faced with unacceptable variations in standards. Pressures for common standards would still exist; local authorities would still operate in the same atmosphere of public opinion, responding to similar political pressures and views of what is acceptable. Common standards would evolve, at a higher level than national minimum standards, and they would have been freely adopted and not imposed from the centre. The doctrine of national minimum standards is highly centralist and undermines local government. It concentrates attention on particular elements in particular services and has no regard for the local impact of the totality of services.

A Separate Block Grant for Education

The Green Paper on *Alternatives to Domestic Rates* (1981, Cmnd 8449) contains an annex on financing the education service either in whole or in part by grant from central government. It discusses various ways in which that could be done.

- Central government could become responsible for the whole of educational expenditure;
- Central government could become responsible for meeting directly a part of educational expenditure, and normally the favoured part is teachers' salaries;
- A special block grant would be paid for education only, based on the same principles as the present block grant for local government services generally.

These proposals have been welcomed, as expected, by many within the education world, and strangely by many outside, who have not fully considered the implications. It has seemed to many that, as if at a stroke, the government has solved both the problems of local government finance and the aspirations of those concerned with education. A heavy burden on the rates appears to have been removed, while at the same time a firm financial base seems to have been provided for the education service. The initially favourable response to these proposals reflects an immediate reaction to an apparently easy way out rather than a careful examination of what would be the consequences of adopting the options.

Some fundamental points must be made:

None of the proposals by itself helps to reduce the burden on the ratepayer

They would only reduce the burden on the ratepayer if the government maintained the present level of grant (or reduced it by less than the amount of any new grant for education). If the government did that there would be an increase in national taxes, which would have to be paid for by some taxpayers. This shift might benefit some ratepayers, but equally some ratepayers would have to pay more in taxation. In practice it is extremely unlikely that the government would be willing to increase national taxation. Thus the proposal would merely mean the replacement of one form of grant by another – hardly the solution to local government's financial problems. Nor would it help education, since the net result would be to make the local authority and the education service even more dependent on grant than now.

This dependence on grant is the source of the current problems of local government finance, and the present proposals would make the local authority, the education service and the ratepayers' fortunes even more dependent on the vagaries of the process of distributing grant.

The proposals are more designed to reduce educational expenditure than increase it

The world of education lives in the belief that if it could only obtain all or a substantial part of its funds direct from central government, then the financial pressures upon the services would disappear or be eased. Central government is clearly seen as likely to be more generous to education than is local government. The reality is very different. The White Paper on the government's expenditure plans (Chancellor of the Exchequer, 1982, Vol. II, p. 39) clearly states that in 1981–2 local government is over-spending by 6 per cent on education. Local government, close to the schools and their needs, has so far been unwilling to impose the degree of cutback on the education service desired by central government. The more the education service becomes directly dependent on central government finance, the more the cuts required by central government are likely to be enforced.

Specific or separate grants will lead to greater central government control over the education service

Central government is not likely to agree to any form of open-ended commitment to pay the bill for all or part of the education service. It will seek to control what it is paying for. The greater the degree of central government control, the less justification there is for local eduation authorities. Yet without local education authorities there is a danger of centrally-imposed rigidity and uniformity in education which few in the service would welcome.

The local education authority would also become simply a pressure group, seeking ever more grant to maximise its expenditure and always blaming the centre for not providing enough to finance the standards thought necessary locally. Thus instead of promoting responsible local decision-making, the proposal is a recipe for irresponsibility.

The proposals are more about the control of maximum standards than the protection and encouragement of minimum standards
The government's favoured proposal is clearly that for a separate block grant for education. The block grant system was introduced by the present government as a means of controlling alleged 'overspending' by particular local authorities. The grant system is designed to discourage high standards of service and an education block grant would bear directly on the education service. It would involve the government specifying for each education authority a figure of grant-related expenditure for the education service. This figure would be what the central government considered should be the level of expenditure of the particular authority. If a local authority decided to spend above that level, various penalties involving loss of grant would be imposed to discourage such expenditure. Those penalties could be made increasingly severe as the central government wished.

The proposal for a separate block grant opens up the possibility that the penalties could be particularly severe against local education authorities perceived as setting too high a standard of service. This assessment is not wild speculation, but a reality, given two critical factors: the large amount of money involved in education and the government's confidence in its capacity to assess the need for educational expenditure in a local authority more accurately than for other services.

The proposals do not provide an easy way out for education. The service should ponder deep and long that at the moment local government is protecting education from the full weight of central government policy for cuts. This protection is no accident, but has arisen because of the very closeness of local councillors to their electorate and because of their sense of responsibility. The more education finance is directly dependent on central government, the more direct and immediate will be the impact of government policy on the education service. Educationists should be wary of the superficial attractions of the government's proposals. Such centralisation could wreak havoc on their service.

Regional Government

Regionalism is back in fashion. Some who seek to decentralise government believe that functions should be allocated to regional rather than to local authorities in England. However, one should be clear that such a move would damage local government. The regional approach is essentially centralist. It represents a top-down paternalism eager to control local government and regarding it as requiring supervision.

Even if, initially, regional governments take over only the existing functions of the present departmental outposts and quangos, they will inevitably intrude into local government responsibilities, since what they are taking over will be the powers to constrain local government. The present supervision will simply be carried out nearer to those being controlled, and it could be even more restrictive because it is closer and fewer authorities are being supervised. There is no need for such supervision, either centrally or regionally. Genuine decentralisation should be to local government. The regional level will still be remote, lacking knowledge of local conditions and needs, and unable to be responsive and sensitive to local circumstances and wishes.

Although regional government may begin with only existing central responsibilities, the momentum of its activities will impel it to seek to acquire from local authorities some of their functions, which it would claim need to be performed over larger areas. Local authorities are now big enough to exercise a wide range of functions and even to take back many lost earlier, such as health, or services placed in quangos like the Manpower Services Commission. Some authorities, like Kent County Council, are bigger in population than many American states, Austrian länder and Swiss cantons. Indeed, British local authorities are generally much larger in their populations than those in Europe, which is one reason why they have so many functions to perform. The advocates of regional government are utopians. They plan decentralisation to bodies that do not now exist, and thus they can impute to regional governments virtues that may not be present in organisations when they are operational. It is more realistic to decentralise to real governments and real people, whose strengths and weaknesses are known, namely local government.

The regionalists hope to create regional political power and political communities as consequences of establishing regional governments: thus conceding that at present there is not, outside Wales and Scotland, much regional consciousness. However, it is doubtful if political communities can be created in such an artificial manner – in a political vacuum. Government needs to grow out of real political communities. Despite the inadequacies of the reorganisation of the structure of local government in the 1970s the present local authorities reflect political communities more than regions. It is significant that those local authorities which are closest to regions in scale – the Greater London Council and metropolitan counties – are the very ones that lack roots in a political community. It is also significant that the areas usually designated as regions represent areas devised by the centre for its administrative convenience. Scotland and Wales represent political communities, but they are more nations than regions, and have a national consciousness and culture. There is no political community or consciousness in the West Midlands or the East Midlands, but there is in cities like Birmingham or Nottingham. To encourage a vigorous non-London culture that will attract talented people, a strengthened local government will be more significant than regional government and the attempt to produce a regional culture.

Regionalists assert that large regions are needed to constitute a powerful check on the centre. But in Europe small local authorities, for instance the communes of France, have great political influence. Political power is not necessarily a result of size: if it were, then the GLC and the metropolitan counties would not be so unpopular and in danger of abolition by central government. Political power arises from the representation of political pressures and of a sense of political community.

Regionalists argue that regional government will produce a more balanced distribution of public expenditure and of economic development. However, the solution to the problem of regional imbalance in the allocation of resources is not regional government. In the competition for resources between regions those already well endowed with advantages will be better able to attract enterprises, unless there are constraints and inducements provided by the centre to steer them elsewhere. Similarly, a strong central government is needed to take an overall view of regional differences and to redirect public expenditure between regions. Regional government is not useful for tackling problems of regional imbalance. Such inter-regional problems require the attention of central government.

An analysis of the usually recommended functions of the regional tier shows that it will exercise over local authorities the controls now operated by central government, and that it will be responsible for the provision of services which at present are the responsibility of local authorities. Because they will be elected, these regional governments, although not representative of any genuine political communities, will feel they have a legitimacy and authority to press their priorities on local authorities. The proposal for regional government is an attempt to constrain the discretion and responsibility of local government. To local authorities it is a proposal for centralisation.

The big-spending functions of present-day government, education, health, housing and the personal social services, are well within the competence of existing local authorities, if only they were freed from central controls and allowed to raise the money to finance them. Some might find it convenient to combine with a neighbouring authority (or authorities) to provide some specialised services, like hospitals. We should beware of arguments based on the need for regions to achieve economies of scale in these activities. There are dis-economies of scale. The more layers of politicians and bureaucrats there are between the electorate and the services they enjoy from the public sector, the more administrative costs and delays are increased, and the less sure you can be that the people are obtaining the services they want.

There is no evidence that bigger is more efficient. It would be certainly less democratic, since regional bureaucrats would be less closely controlled by elected councillors, more remote from the people and in no way as accountable, responsible and responsive to local communities as are existing local authorities.

Meddling MPs

A report on London's transport from the House of Commons Select Committee on Transport (House of Commons Transport Committee, 1982) highlights a disturbing trend for local government. Here is a committee, with only one representative from a London constituency, investigating a topic that is not the responsibility of any central government department and recommending that a non-elected quango should take over public transport from the elected Greater London Council. No wonder the Transport Secretary jumped in with an exceptionally quick welcome. It was a triumph for centralism.

This episode illustrates an increasingly significant development. Over the years, it is often argued, the power of the executive has grown too quickly, and therefore the House needs to redress the balance and to strengthen its instruments of control. The favoured device has been the select committee, fourteen of which now shadow most government departments. This present select committee system was introduced in 1979 by the then Leader of the House, Norman St

John-Stevas. Reviewing the first years of the new select committee system, those who were sceptical of the changes have seen their premonitions justified.

The terms of reference were too broad. They empower the examination of government departments, their policy, administration and expenditure, as well as the work of their associated public bodies. This wide remit means that the committees have no sharp focus and no discipline to guide their inquiries, with the result that they vary in what and how they investigate. Some have turned their attention from Whitehall to investigate the responsibilities of local government, for example sale of council houses and the provision of education. Once, select committees acted as watchdogs over the civil service, probing the administration and implementation of policy. Now, with extensive terms of reference, such investigations are neglected for more glamorous forays. The new select committees have let the civil service off a hook.

A desirable reform would be to revise the terms of reference of the select committees, to confine them to investigate the administration of policy. With this sharper focus their inquiries would be more intense, structured and systematic, and ultimately more effective than their present dispersed efforts. Those concerned about the need to provide an adequate check on central bureaucracy should be worried that select committees' grip on the civil service has been relaxed through a dissipation of their challenges.

Select committees should also not be diverted to investigate local authorities, since Parliament has deliberately set up local authorities not to be as fully accountable to Parliament as departments through their ministers. For the performance of local government functions local officials are, in our constitution, responsible to their own councils of members elected by local voters. Yet MPs have sought to extend Commons' scrutiny over local government activities, hearing evidence from the local authority associations and probing what happens within local authorities.

The associations have been asked for information about how select committees can be more involved in the scrutiny of local government expenditure – another example of them being distracted from their key task of investigating central government bureaucracy. Select committees should not seek to monitor local government expenditure, if financed from rates, but should concentrate on scrutiny of central government grant, for instance, whether the proposed level of grant is sufficient to enable local authorities to carry out their statutory responsibilities, and whether it is compatible with the government's macro-economic objectives and plan for public expenditure. Parliament needs to scrutinise the methodology of the grant system, in particular the way the grant-related expenditure assessments are calculated and assigned to individual local authorities. It should probe the process by which the executive decides what local government should spend. It should examine whether the methods of measuring needs and resources make sense, and whether the eventual grant has properly taken account of inflation and wage settlements. It should focus its attention on the activities of the executive in making the Rate Support Grant Order, on the objectives of the minister and on whether his chosen means are appropriate. In this way Parliament would ensure that the Secretary of State was truly accountable to Parliament, and not interfere in the responsibilities of local government.

When select committees have reported on local authority responsibilities they have invariably recommended an increase in the powers of the central civil service through the imposition of national standards and controls, which undermine local accountability. If MPs really were serious about the need to check the central executive, they would welcome local government as an ally, and recommend the decentralisation of more functions to it. By maximising its autonomy and by promoting genuine local accountability local government can be made a significant counterweight to the central bureaucracy.

It may be thought that the July 1982 report of the Environment Select Committee (House of Commons Environment Committee, 1982) on methods of financing local government contradicts these arguments, since it promotes the welfare of local government. However, the report makes its main impact because it challenges the enclosed world of civil service advice, especially on the administrative possibility of a local income tax.

Another tendency of MPs has distracted their attention away from the civil service and has actually increased the interference of central bureaucracy over local government. Over the years MPs have tended increasingly to act as welfare workers for their constituents, personally handling their complaints, and not just against central government. Some MPs have become glorified local councillors, undertaking business that should properly be left to local politicians. By passing on constituents' complaints about local government to ministers, through letters, parliamentary questions and points in debate, MPs engage ministers' attention, and that of their civil servants, in local government responsibilities. MPs have become a pressure for centralisation, encouraging departments to be involved in local affairs. While MPs are so absorbed in these multifarious local issues, they are ignoring national concerns.

MPs should, therefore, exercise a self-denying ordinance of restraint and ensure that local councillors, and not themselves, handle local government business and that they concentrate on national issues. Local councils themselves should be more ready to protest and resist encroachment on local responsibilities by MPs. Part of the trouble arises from the fact that there are too many MPs, with the result that many MPs have no satisfying role to perform. So, they immerse themselves in select committees or dabble in local matters. MPs should not seek to expand their control over everything or they will end up controlling nothing. Above all, MPs should be checking national bureaucracy. Select committees are an appropriate instrument for that task. A check on national bureaucracy can also be provided by a strong system of local government.

12 The Way Ahead for Local Government Finance

(with Tony Travers)

Introduction

At a time when local government finance is in crisis, when central–local relations are a major constitutional question and when there is widespread agreement that a fundamental solution is required, a Green Paper (Secretaries of State for the Environment, for Scotland and for Wales, 1981) is produced which focuses on domestic rates, which constitute less than 20 per cent of the income of local authorities. Fundamental issues are missed by this concentration on only an aspect of the problem. The heart of the problem of local government finance is that about five times as much revenue is obtained from taxes that do not bear on the local elector (national taxation and the non-domestic rate) as from the one tax that does – the domestic rate. Even if a new tax replaces domestic rates, that crucial problem remains unchanged. The government must not pursue such a partial approach. It should resolve the main issues. It should be concerned not simply with alternatives to domestic rates, but with the basis of local government finance and the need to strengthen local accountability. Like the Layfield Report (1976) it should consider:

- the desired relationship between central and local government;
- the requirements of local accountability;
- the form and nature of grant;
- alternatives to non-domestic rates;
- the scope for fees and charges;
- appropriate taxation to promote local accountability;
- the relationship between the various sources of local government income.

The overall tone of the Green Paper is negative, perhaps natural in a document intended to provoke discussion. It presents different views and emphasises difficulties so that no one later may allege he was not warned. This approach tends to exaggerate administrative difficulties. The proper response for government is to be positive and constructive, and not to allow administrative problems to be an insuperable obstacle to achieving what the government believes to be right. A government determined to solve the problem of local government finance and to strengthen local democracy will select the option which really enhances local responsibility and accountability. Administrative factors should not be allowed to frustrate political will.

In devising a system of local government finance the first step is to decide the relationship between central and local government it is to serve. The present arrangements are a hotchpotch of provisions which lead to confusion and ambiguity. They do not enable responsibility to be clearly located. Both central and local government can claim not to be responsible for local government expenditure and its financing. The former will argue that it distributes grant to local authorities in the form of a block general grant without strings attached and that it does not directly control the rates levied by local authorities. They in turn reply that they are so constrained by central controls and mandatory obligations that their expenditure is already committed and that the rates are determined more by central decisions and the amount of grant than by their own decisions on local priorities. Thus each side engages in a ritual of passing the buck: none is prepared to say 'we are responsible'. This evasion of responsibility, and hence accountability, for huge sums of taxpayers' and ratepayers' money is a national scandal. It is dressed up in the rhetoric of partnership and sharing responsibility. But the reality of this joint responsibility is that no one is responsible. So, the major choice for the country is to decide where it wants to locate the main responsibility for the expenditure and financing of local government. It can be with either central or local government. If the case for local government already stated is accepted, then the answer must be local government, for without clear responsibility for expenditure decisions, there is no basis for local government as opposed to local administration.

In seeking to establish a system of local government finance to sustain responsible local government a vital principle needs to determine all elements of the package. Decision-making in government, by councillors and voters, cannot be responsible if it is about expenditure only. Decisions on expenditure need to be intimately linked with decisions on how to finance that expenditure, so that those who decide to spend more have at the very same time to accept the consequences of that decision and impose higher taxes, while those who decide to have lower taxes have at the very same time to accept the consequences of that decision with cuts in services. Local authorities cannot be regarded as responsible bodies if they simply spend money that they have not raised from their own voters. If they are too dependent on grants they will become mere pressure groups for their localities, always asking for higher grants and blaming the central government for not providing enough grant for the desired levels of local services. Thus responsible local authorities need to raise the bulk of their income from their local voters, and not to rely on government grants. It is on the critical local balance between local expenditure and local taxation that local accountability must rest.

The Main Features of the Local Government Financial System – the Basic Approach

The fatal defect in local accountability at present is that nearly five times as much revenue is drawn by local government from taxes that do not bear clearly and directly on local electors (from government grant and the non-domestic rate) as from the one tax that bears directly on some, not all, local voters (the domestic rate). Only about 8 per cent of local authority income is provided by ratepayers who actually turn out to vote in local elections. This calculation is based on the assumption that somewhat under half of the householders, who provide the 17 per cent of local income raised by rates, vote in local elections. To achieve genuine local accountability the local government financial system should be recast to ensure that local authorities draw the bulk of their income from their own local taxpayers and voters, and that the latter are aware that they are paying their taxes to support local government services. Such an approach requires two major changes:

(i)   a reduction in government grant, and
(ii)   local taxation that can provide a big enough yield to finance most local government activities, that is perceptible to local voters as taxation for local government and is borne directly by them.

A commitment to such an approach rules out such taxes as sales taxes or petrol taxes, which do not necessarily bear on local voters, and reliance on many small taxes, which will be a complex tangle, not clearly perceptible to the electorate and incapable of raising the income required. The only serious starting candidate as a replacement for or as a supplement to rates is local income tax.

A commitment to this approach also rules out three other courses of action, widely supported and referred to in the Green Paper:

(i)   *Assigned revenues* would be a source of revenue little different

from central government grant, since the local authority would
not be able to determine their level. They would break the link
of accountability between councils and their electors and not
encourage responsible decision-making by local government.

(ii) *Separate block grant* for particular services, like education, *or
specific grants* for such services or parts of such services, would
also be a major shift to central control, since the freedom of
local authorities to determine their spending priorities would
be much reduced in both types of grant. The centre would also
face the controversial and complex task of determining for each
authority precise levels of expenditure and grant.

(iii) *Transfer to the centre* of the responsibility for the cost of the
service, either wholly (e.g. education) or in part (e.g. teachers'
salaries), would also be a major diminution of local government
responsibility. It would encourage irresponsibility in local
authorities since it would be an incentive for them to increase
their demand for expenditure and then to blame the centre for
not providing sufficient grant. Such transfers would diminish
the capacity of local government to be genuine community
government, since it would no longer be able to consider the
total effect on its locality of a wide range of services, to examine
the relationships between them, to decide on priorities, and to
provide that mixture of services that most fits the needs and
wishes of that particular area. If responsibility for only part of a
service were transferred, then local authorities would not be
fully in control of the service and its development. Central and
local government would blame each other for everything that
went wrong.

The Centre's Functions

The central government should set a stable framework for a local
government financial system that promotes local accountability. For
the centre to have adequate powers to manage the economy as a
whole it should exercise tight control over the borrowing of local
authorities. They should not be allowed, for instance, to borrow for
current expenditure and engage in deficit financing. Their borrowing
should be for capital expenditure. Central government's control over
borrowing can adopt different approaches. The first is for the centre
to control local authorities' capital expenditure, either their specific
projects or longer-term programmes. This method is centralist, since
central departments can easily become involved in scrutiny and
approval of local government's plans for particular services, not to
preserve an authority's creditworthiness but to influence its

functions, like education, housing or social services. This type of control will also cover more than borrowing since it will encompass capital expenditure, however it is financed, even from current revenue or by leasing. An alternative is for central government merely to control borrowing.

The decentralist method, whilst preserving the central control necessary for macro-economic management, is to let local authorities borrow in the market, subject to the discipline of the market and interest rates, and to enable the Treasury to raise or lower the price of their borrowing, depending on the Treasury's assessment of the public sector borrowing requirement and the state of the money markets, by means of a regulator, which would require local authorities to finance stated and varying proportions of their capital expenditure from current income. This second approach combines the maximum local responsibility and accountability with the control essential to enable the central government to carry out its national role of managing the economy overall.

The centre must also control the grant it provides to local government. Such national decisions on borrowing and grant, but only those decisions, should appear in the annual Public Expenditure White Paper. The central government would be held clearly responsible for such decisions. It should not involve itself in controlling expenditure by local government, capital or current, as long as that expenditure is financed by local authorities out of local taxes levied on their local voters. There would thus be a clear separation between public expenditure for which central government is responsible and accountable, and that for which local government is responsible and accountable.

Grant

Local government should be cured of its addiction to high grant. The level of over 50 per cent is too large for responsible local government. Grant should be reduced certainly to no more than 40 per cent of local government rate fund income (the minimum figure chosen by the Layfield Committee as being compatible with existing equalisation objectives), and preferably much lower, ideally below 30 per cent. Grant should no longer be expected to perform the multifarious functions at present laid upon it, to penalise or reward specific authorities or to subsidise certain categories of local tax-payer. Grant at present equalises resources as measured by rateable value in relation to a government assessment of need. Grant should in future equalise resources on the basis of average incomes, which is the best test of capacity to pay local taxes.

Some may object to equalising resources on the basis of average incomes because such figures are not maintained for local authority areas. That defect should be remedied at once. It is very serious that such vital social statistics should not be available and as a result there is inadequate evidence about the impact of existing grant systems. Of course, with local income tax such information would be automatically available.

There are obvious dangers if in addition grant equalises in relation to the government's assessment of need. Such equalisation opens the door to centralisation. There has to be a central assessment of need, which undermines the whole rationale of local government, namely that local authorities are the best judges of local needs. The centre cannot adequately assess the needs of many and varied local authorities. When it tries to, it enters into a complex process fraught with controversy, in which the main protagonists are the few bureaucrats who can understand the technical jargon. The system is unstable, since each year in response to complaints about the measurement of need the factors will change with consequent unsettling alterations in grant received. These objections would not arise if the equalisation scheme were devised and operated by local authorities themselves, even if it involved an element of central grant. Rules could be drawn up specifying the extent and conditions of such arrangements. If the dangers of centralisation are perceived as of paramount importance, then the very notion of a needs grant will be rejected. However, we recognise that some trade-off between the certainty of avoiding centralisation and a measure of equalisation of spending need may be thought desirable; then such a grant should be made simple and stable, and the legislation drafted in such a way as to preclude ministerial interference that undermines local responsibility.

It may be suggested that the best objective factor is population, and that therefore grant should be based on *per capita* population. However, such a grant would be simply a general subsidy, which should be unnecessary given adequate sources of local revenue. The promotion of local responsibility and accountability requires that grants as general subsidies should be abolished.

A grant of only 30 per cent, or lower, would not have to attempt to be as precise as one of 60 per cent. Because grant would represent a much smaller part of councils' income than is presently the case, it could be a broader and cruder exercise, more simple to operate and far more comprehensible than the present system.

It is possible to provide for equalisation without any grant at all, through a 'pooling' arrangement. In such a scheme authorities with above average incomes would use their resources to make up the incomes of those below the average. However, local authorities might object to what they would regard as a clawback or penalty, visibly being taken from them to assist others.

Non-Domestic Rate

Local accountability would be strengthened by the transfer of the non-domestic rate to central government as a national tax. This tax is not suitable as a tax for local government. It is not paid directly by voters in the locality. Non-domestic rate is probably not borne by industry and commerce, but by those who buy goods and services from those who pay the non-domestic rate. Transfer to the centre would enable the national government to plan its industrial fiscal policies more effectively. It would simplify and facilitate the process of distribution of the equalisation grant. At present great disparities in the resources of different local authorities arise from the varying amounts of non-domestic rateable property they possess. Average incomes do not vary between local authorities to such a degree. Therefore, the process of redistribution based on average incomes would entail a simpler process and a lower grant than the present based on rateable values.

The present non-domestic ratepayers would still be financing local government from their national taxes fed to local government through grant, while a system of charging for services directly provided by local authorities would forge a clear and direct link between local government and industry, commerce and also agriculture which at present escapes paying rates on agricultural land and farm buildings. Industry and commerce would not escape from the responsibility of helping to finance local government, even if non-domestic rates became a national tax.

Domestic Rates

Domestic rates should be reformed, not abolished. They are an ideal local government tax, encouraging local accountability. They are perceptible; bear on local voters; are hard to evade; with a predictable yield; cheap to collect; progressive for low-income earners, proportional for the middle-income groups and regressive only at the top end. Property cries out to be taxed; most countries in the world tax property; if it were abolished as a local government tax, it would not be long before the Treasury took it on as a national tax. The replacement of domestic rates by local income tax or a sales tax would be a partly regressive step, hitting some low-income groups who are now helped by rate rebates to pay their rates. With local income tax (at least with personal allowances at their present level) or a sales tax they would face higher taxation without corresponding allowances. For some low-income earners rates are more related to their ability to pay than are income tax or a sales tax.

Domestic rating needs to be reformed. First, the basis of assessment should be changed from rental to capital valuation. There is more evidence now of capital than of rental values; capital valuation would be more comprehensible to the public, especially if the valuation were related as closely as possible to the purchase price; and it would be fairer, since at present a £200,000 house is not assessed for rating purposes at ten times the value of a house of £20,000. Rating would be more clearly related to ability to pay. The wealthy living in more valuable property would be paying a fairer share to local government. Secondly, regular revaluations are needed to up-date and maintain the tax base. With capital valuation each sales transaction would provide evidence for the valuers and could be used to determine the rateable value. Thus rates could become a buoyant tax. Capital valuation should provide sufficient evidence for valuers to speed up the process of valuation, so that it could take place every three years. There is also a case for removing valuation from the Inland Revenue and putting it in the hands of an independent body, not distracted by other duties or at the mercy of a central government reluctant to allow revaluation to take place.

Local Income Tax

With the retention of domestic rates, the transfer of non-domestic rates to the centre and the reduction of grant, a new source of local revenue is required to replace the lost income. Reviews of possible options suggest that only one tax meets the two critical criteria of raising a substantial yield and promoting local accountability by bearing on local voters, and that is a local income tax.

It would ensure that the earning non-householders, around 10 million people who at present pay income tax but are not directly ratepayers, make a direct and visible contribution to the financing of local government. At present they help to finance local government expenditure through their income tax and other national taxes fed into grant. But they do not realise that they are financing local government. With a local income tax their contributions to local government would be explicit. They would be more aware that they were financing local government expenditure and take a greater interest in how the money was spent. Public participation and electoral concern would be encouraged.

Local income tax is viable: the working experience of other countries, in Scandinavia and the USA, shows that LIT is a practical proposition. The Layfield Committee on Local Government Finance (1976) worked out a scheme in collaboration with the Inland Revenue, which is administratively feasible. Other schemes have been suggested in the Green Paper and elsewhere. What is necessary to introduce LIT is political will on the part of the government of the day. Administrative problems are not or should not be an obstacle to the introduction of a local income tax. A clear political commitment should be made to a local income tax and the whole effort of Inland Revenue and local authorities can then be devoted to resolving the administrative problems involved. The Layfield investigations showed what could be achieved by positive examination. We consider that it should be possible to introduce a local income tax within the lifetime of a Parliament, but even if that were not possible, the commitment should be made. Any other course means further delay. If the commitment had been made at the time of the Layfield Report, a local income tax would now be in operation.

The Layfield plan envisaged that Inland Revenue would be responsible for the assessment of liability to tax and for the collection of the tax, thus making use of the national machinery, but that each local authority would set its own rate of tax. There is no point in having LIT if a single uniform rate of tax is prescribed nationally. Local responsibility requires that local authorities should be able to vary the rate of tax. It would be levied on taxpayers on the basis of their place of residence, so as to fall on local voters. The local authority would report its tax rate to the Inland Revenue, which would then collect it, using appropriate codes and taxation tables for PAYE taxpayers.

Some objections to LIT need to be countered. It may be argued that no national government would ever allow an important fiscal instrument for managing the economy to slip from its hands and local authorities to vary the rate of tax. This Treasury view is just the centralist orthodoxy that should be challenged. Other countries run more healthy economies than ours without resort to the means of intervention deployed by the British Treasury. In any case it would still retain the wide range of other taxes, including the non-domestic rate, which it could use in any exercise of fine-tuning the economy or to adjust tax burdens in the light of local government decisions on the income tax. Sharing this tax should pose no major problem for central management of the economy. Tax sharing in other countries is common and presents no serious problems for fiscal management.

It may be objected that the cost of LIT is too great. Layfield's investigations (which if more time had been available could have been taken further) brought the cost down from Inland Revenue's initially inflated estimate to £50 million public and £50 million employers' costs at 1976 prices (1981/2 prices £110 million public and £110 million private costs). Later studies suggest that further reductions can be made through computerisation at Inland Revenue or the introduction of a self-assessment system, as in the USA. It should be noted that the collection costs of LIT would be closer to that for rates, if regular revaluations for the latter were carried out, since the failure to carry out revaluations has kept the costs of rates artificially low. The introduction of LIT will incur extra costs, but that may well be a price worth paying to establish a genuine system of local responsibility as a counter-balance to centralisation, which in the end should result in a more effective financial discipline on local government expenditure and a wiser use of resources.

It may be objected that LIT can never be as perceptible to the local voter as domestic rates. But LIT as a replacement for grant would undoubtedly be more perceptible locally than the 13p of income tax used currently to make up the grant total. Even with payment through PAYE LIT would bring it home to many more people than at present that they were contributing large sums to local government. Local authorities would have to inform their voters of the rate of LIT, and there would be considerable publicity given to the decision setting the tax rate. The amount taken for local government would also be indicated on wages and salaries slips. Indeed, the citizen might be more aware of the local income tax payment than of his national contribution. This form of local income tax would be viable. It is not the only possible form. Perceptibility would be increased by a move from PAYE to self-assessment and 'year end' schemes – as it would by a shift to collection by the local authority through lump-sum payments. It would be possible to base a local income tax on local authority collection either with self-assessment or using figures supplied by Inland Revenue. It would also be possible for Inland Revenue to collect local income tax at a national average rate with local authorities responsible for direct collection and rebating the difference. With each option there are different associated costs and benefits. What is required is a decision in principle on a local income tax and a quick, detailed and positive investigation of the administrative implications of the different approaches.

It may be objected that the introduction of LIT will mark an increase in direct taxation. It would probably do so, if LIT were to replace domestic rates, but not if LIT replaced grant and non-domestic rates as a local tax. In fact there need be no increase in the total burden of direct taxation. No one's income tax as a whole need necessarily rise, since the national income tax can be reduced by the corresponding reduction in grant and the amount of the non-domestic rate. Each individual will merely pay in LIT a part of what previously he was paying as national income tax.

It may be objected that a poll tax would be a better substitute. But a poll tax will be a tax on the right to participate in the democratic process; it will be a disincentive to register on the electoral roll; it will be costly to administer and check up on evasion and removals; it will be a highly regressive tax, taking a bigger proportion of the incomes of the poorer than of the richer. To replace domestic rates a flat-rate sum of £120 a year will be needed, with £240 required from the average household of two adults. It will not reflect ability to pay, unless rebates related to income are introduced. If one is prepared to set up the administrative machinery to operate this tax in this way, then it would be better to operate a local income tax, which automatically relates to ability to pay.

The Options

The main advantage of the scheme outlined above is that it improves accountability while making the operation of local authority finance more rational and comprehensible. A much larger proportion of local spending would be met from local sources bearing clearly on local voters. Non-domestic rates would be a matter for central government to decide, as is appropriate for a tax on industrial and commercial costs.

The proposals have the additional advantage that they need not lead to a net increase in income tax. This can be demonstrated by Figures 12.1 and 12.2. Figure 12.1 shows the flows of resources from individuals and corporations into local and central government (in a somewhat simplified form). Flows of resources affecting local government directly are shown by the money amounts in brackets. Thus, the figure of £5,176 million by the 'rates' line from individuals implies a total rate payment by householders of £5,176 million in 1982–3. Local government's total income is shown at the bottom right-hand corner of the figure, broken down by source.

Figure 12.2 shows the flows of resources if the scheme outlined in this chapter were adopted. The flow of non-domestic rates from corporations to local government (in Figure 12.1) is diverted into central government, thus reducing central government's revenue requirements. At the same time, the grant paid by the centre to local authorities is cut by £5,392 million. This reduction is made on the assumption that in the new scheme grant would no longer be used as a simple subsidy to local taxation and that the 'equalisation' requirements, if any, would be very considerably reduced in the new system to 30 per cent, although the precise proportion would be open for legislation to determine. A truly local system of local government requires the smallest possible grant. However, the size of the grant reduction in this Figure does not affect the net tax and revenue changes in the system.

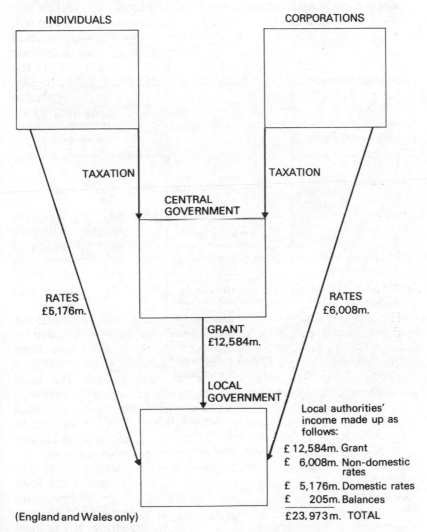

Figure 12.1   *1982–3 Position*

Central government's revenue has now been increased by £6,008 million (non-domestic rates), while the demands on it have been reduced by £5,392 million. This would allow a reduction of £11,400

million in central government income tax. A local income tax could
then make up the £11,400 million reduction in local authority
income. This is represented by the new line from 'individuals' to
'local government'. As in Figure 12.1, local authority total income is
shown in the bottom right-hand corner of the Figure.

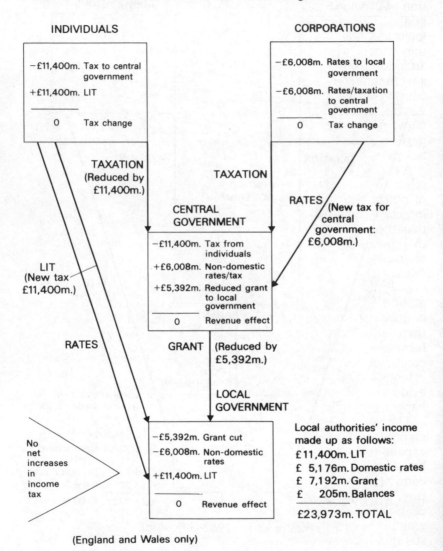

Figure 12.2   *The Preferred Solution*

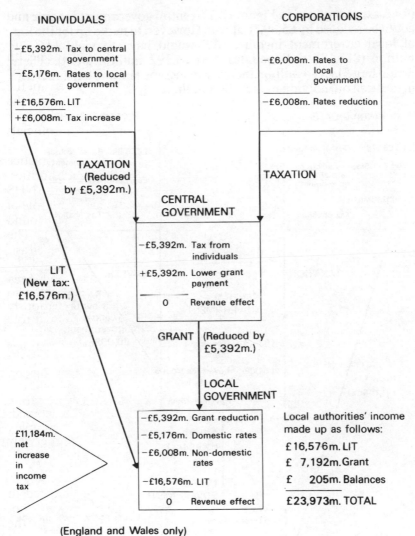

INDIVIDUALS

−£5,392m. Tax to central government
−£5,176m. Rates to local government
+£16,576m. LIT
+£6,008m. Tax increase

CORPORATIONS

−£6,008m. Rates to local government
−£6,008m. Rates reduction

TAXATION
(Reduced by £5,392m.)

TAXATION

CENTRAL GOVERNMENT

−£5,392m. Tax from individuals
+£5,392m. Lower grant payment
0 Revenue effect

LIT
(New tax: £16,576m.)

GRANT (Reduced by £5,392m.)

LOCAL GOVERNMENT

−£5,392m. Grant reduction
−£5,176m. Domestic rates
−£6,008m. Non-domestic rates
−£16,576m. LIT
0 Revenue effect

Local authorities' income made up as follows:
£16,576m. LIT
£ 7,192m. Grant
£ 205m. Balances
£23,973m. TOTAL

£11,184m. net increase in income tax

(England and Wales only)

Figure 12.3 *No Rates Solution*

Having looked at the solution outlined in this paper, we turn to other suggested changes. Figure 12.3 shows the flows of resources in a system where rates were abolished for both householders and non-domestic ratepayers. Local government would lose £11,184 million in income from rates. If grant were to be reduced by £5,392 million (for reasons outlined in Figure 12.2), central government income tax could be reduced by £5,392 million. However, to make up for the loss of local government income, LIT would have to yield £16,576 million (£11,184 million rates plus £5,392 million grant). There would be a £11,184 million increase in income tax, and a net increase in taxation on individuals of £6,008 million.

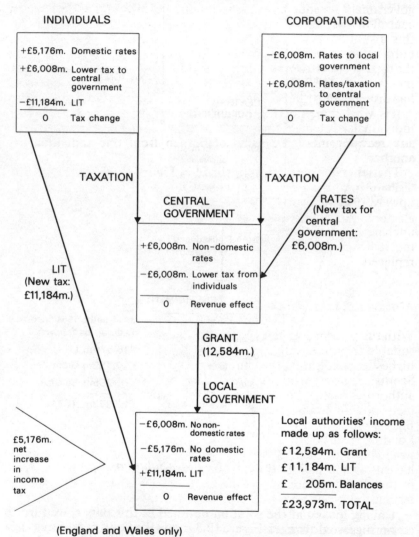

INDIVIDUALS

+£5,176m. Domestic rates
+£6,008m. Lower tax to central government
−£11,184m. LIT
_____
0   Tax change

CORPORATIONS

−£6,008m. Rates to local government
+£6,008m. Rates/taxation to central government
_____
0   Tax change

TAXATION

TAXATION

CENTRAL GOVERNMENT

RATES (New tax for central government: £6,008m.)

+£6,008m. Non-domestic rates
−£6,008m. Lower tax from individuals
_____
0   Revenue effect

LIT (New tax: £11,184m.)

GRANT (12,584m.)

LOCAL GOVERNMENT

−£6,008m. No non-domestic rates
−£5,176m. No domestic rates
+£11,184m. LIT
_____
0   Revenue effect

£5,176m. net increase in income tax

Local authorities' income made up as follows:

£12,584m. Grant
£11,184m. LIT
£   205m. Balances
_____
£23,973m. TOTAL

(England and Wales only)

Figure 12.4   *No Domestic Rates Solution (Non-Domestic Rates to Central Government)*

Figure 12.4 looks at the position if domestic rates only were to be abolished – a solution which has found much favour with politicians of all parties. It is assumed that in such a situation non-domestic rates would be paid to central government (it being unlikely that the government would allow local authorities to tax companies without a corresponding tax on individuals). This would increase central government revenue by £6,008 million, which would allow a cut in central income tax. If grant were to be held at its current level (again, this assumption is not important to the net flows of tax and tax burden), there would need to be a LIT yielding £11,184 million (i.e. the total of domestic and non-domestic rates). This would imply a net increase in income tax of about £5,176 million, though, because rates had disappeared, there would be no net increase in tax on individuals.

It is worth remembering that although there may be no net effect on individuals of changes in the distribution of taxation, there will, with any rearrangement, be shifts of burden from one individual to another.

The scheme proposed, as outlined in Figure 12.2, has the advantages of producing no net change in income tax, unless so willed, upward or downward, by local councils accountable to their local electors, and of leaving the tax system as a whole comparatively unchanged. The other options, involving the abolition of a tax, would inevitably lead to greater upheaval because the income lost has to be replaced.

Allocation of Taxes Between the Tiers

With the present two-tier system of local government LIT would be suitable for those authorities responsible for the services with the highest expenditure – the shire counties, metropolitan districts and Scottish regions; while domestic rates would be suitable for local authorities with the less expensive functions – shire districts, metropolitan counties and Scottish districts. London presents the biggest problem, because of the differences between inner and outer London. The position of the Inner London Education Authority would have to be clarified. The objective is for each local authority to have its own local tax, either LIT or domestic rates, and not to engage in the complications of sharing taxes or of precepting which blur responsibility and accountability.

A different structure of local government based on unitary authorities would make such an allocation unnecessary. We consider such a reorganisation in the last chapter; but even if that were not to take place, new taxation powers should be introduced. The first priority is to reform the present financial system and not delay it into the future. One should be wary of opponents of LIT who seek to block its introduction by proposing a major reorganisation first. Reform of the present financial system must not be delayed, otherwise there may be no local government to be reformed. It will have been transformed into an agency of central government.

Summary of the Seven Main Proposals

1   There should be a clear separation between expenditure for which the central government is responsible and accountable and that for which local government is responsible and accountable.
2   The centre should control its grant and borrowing by local government. It should not seek to control the current and capital expenditure of local government as long as it is financed out of taxes levied by local authorities on their local voters, without resort to deficit financing and borrowing.
3   Grant should be reduced to below 30 per cent of local government rate-fund income, compared to the 52·8 per cent at present.
4   The non-domestic rate should be transferred to the centre, since it is not appropriate as a local government tax. It does not encourage local accountability, and complicates the process of equalising the resources of local authorities.
5   Domestic rating should be retained as an ideal local government tax, but assessments should be based on capital not rental valuation and subject to a regular, at least every three years', revaluation.
6   To make up for the reduction of grant to below 30 per cent, and for the loss of non-domestic rating, local government should receive as a supplement to domestic rating the proceeds of local income tax, collected through the Inland Revenue on the basis of place of residence. The rate of tax is to be set by the local authority, which will inform Inland Revenue of the rate.
7   If a two-tier structure of local government is retained, then LIT will be used to finance the big-spending authorities and domestic rates the low-spending, so that each authority is allocated its own visible local tax.

13 A Charter for Local Government

The Original Proposal

Governments of different parties have contributed to the erosion of local responsibility. Powers taken by one government are used by governments of different political persuasion. The powers taken by this government may be used by future governments. The very flexibility of those powers opens up new uncertainties.

Local authorities need protection in the exercise of their responsibility, and in their relations with central government, against the erosion of their position. The relationship between central government and local authorities should be recognised as a critical constitutional relationship even without a written constitution. The moment has surely come to pause and take stock. The situation changes too rapidly. Too much is at stake. A constitutional relationship under threat requires protection. A Charter for local government could provide the basis for that protection.

A Charter would set out the necessary conditions for the operations of effective local government:

- local elections
- procedures for public accountability
- independent and substantial sources of income
- clear areas for independent action
- certainty of powers, duties and the conditions under which they would be exercised.

The Charter would specify the principles which should guide central government intervention in the affairs and activities of local authorities. Examples could include:

1 Central government's policies for the services for which local authorities are responsible should be achieved by legislation, laying down duties for all authorities rather than by ministerial powers that can be exercised in different ways against different authorities.
2 Central government should aim at creating a stable and certain environment for local authority decision-making.
3 Where central government has power to specify conditions for

local authority decision-making, those conditions should be specified prior to the local authority decision-making and not altered retrospectively.

4   The overall aim of central government should be to increase rather than decrease the area of discretion at the level of the local authority.

The proposal for a Charter is to stimulate a debate, which should take place before further damage is done. The moment has come to consider principles, for constitutional issues are at stake. A proposal for a Charter may be condemned as mere words. Words are certainly what a Charter consists of, but words are important. The time has come for principles, and principles are expressed in words. Principles provide a marking point against which further challenge and change can be judged. The principles, once recorded, provide a measuring rod for proposals for change in central–local relations and for the gradual and subtle change that derives from changing attitudes.

A Standing Commission on Central–Local Relations could report on particular proposals and on gradual change. Local authorities may well argue against such a proposal as yet another body to inquire into local government. But what is envisaged is a commission to inquire not into local government, but into the relationship between central government and local authorities. Local government can benefit from such an institution. What is envisaged is not a commission with power to impose, but power to expose. The Charter would give it a measuring rod. A commission is not essential to the proposal. The proposal for a Charter can stand on its own, to mark deeply the relationship between central government and local authorities.

It may be said that central government would never agree to such a proposal. That may be, but as the relationship between central government and local government worsens, central government may face a choice between ever more frantic measures in a deteriorating relationship or an attempt to achieve a new and a constructive relationship. Constructive proposals are required. A proposal for a Charter might well be rejected by central government. Yet it need not be. The government itself may wish an end to policies that lead to confrontation. The proposal for a Charter can focus attention on the critical issue of central–local relations. That relationship is moving to even greater uncertainty and even greater crisis.

Further Thoughts

In a country without a written constitution, constitutional changes can take place imperceptibly. Apparently minor and administrative changes can accumulate into a fundamental constitutional change, unnoticed until too late. The relationship between central and local government is of constitutional importance, since local councils are the only elected authorities apart from the House of Commons itself. Through direct election, both central and local government possess an authority and legitimacy denied to other organisations. The relationship between the two, therefore, is a basic feature of the constitution, and changes to it should not be made without explicit appreciation of their consequences.

But at present such changes can happen without adequate consideration of their implications. For instance, few MPs and Peers have been aware of the significance of the provisions in the Local Government (Miscellaneous Provisions) (Scotland) Act, which wrought a constitutional change in central–local relations and may set the pattern for future legislation applying to England and Wales. It allows central government to withdraw grant from local authorities whose estimates of future expenditure seem to the Secretary of State to be excessive or unreasonable, while preventing them from using other sources of income, e.g. the rates, to replace the lost grant. Thus the centre is given virtually direct control over an individual local authority's expenditure.

The Local Government, Planning and Land Act 1980 also produced a constitutional shift. The centre moved from a concern with the total of the aggregate expenditure of local government to a concern for the spending of particular authorities.

A Charter is required to specify the principles which should guide central government's interventions in the activities of local authorities. It should set out the conditions for effective local government and act as a measuring rod for assessing changes in central–local relations. What is needed now is discussion about the contents of such a Charter, and whether they should be expressed in positive or negative terms. Positive statements may be too general as guides to action. They may usefully form an opening passage of pious intention, but far more significant will be the listing of activities which should not occur.

For example, it may be *positively* asserted that central government's policies for the services for which local authorities are responsible should be expressed in legislation that lays down duties for all local authorities. The *negative*, and more specific, formulation would be that the centre should not promote its policies for local government services by ministerial directions, such as when a minister can act 'if he thinks fit'; or discriminate between local authorities by exercising powers in different ways against different local authorities; or have to approve or disapprove of local authority plans and schemes unless they impinge on other local authorities.

Positively, it may assert that the centre should set broad national policy objectives and leave local authorities to be responsible for their achievement. The *negative* formulation might be that the centre should not intervene in local administration, which affects only that local authority, or lay down minimum input standards for service provision.

Positively, it may assert that the centre should create a stable and certain environment, a minimum framework for local authority decision-making. The *negative* formulation might be that the centre should not specify conditions for local authority decision-making once the year in which the decisions are to be made has begun, nor retrospectively.

Positively, it may assert that the centre, for macro-economic purposes, should be concerned with its own expenditure, the level of grant and with local government borrowing. The *negative* formulation might be that the centre should not be concerned with the total of local government expenditure, expenditure by particular authorities and on particular services, and with the burden on local taxpayers.

Positively, it may assert that the centre should use grant for equalising the resources of local authorities. The *negative* formulation might be that grant should not be over 30 per cent of total relevant local expenditure, and should not be used to subsidise classes of local taxpayer, to influence the provision of local services, to reward or punish individual local authorities or as a macro-economic regulator.

So far the terms have been conceived as erecting barriers to protect local government from central erosion of its responsibility. The Charter would also have to lay down (a) conditions for effective local responsibility, such as regulations for local elections and procedures for public accountability; and (b) constraints on local authorities to stop them encroaching on each other's and on central responsibilities.

For instance, there is a need to curb local authorities from seeking central intervention in local services through directions, guidance, circulars and letters, and from involvement in the PESC process unless to provide information for forecasting. The Charter might also cover mutual obligations. For instance, if the centre can call for information of various kinds from local authorities, so they should have the right to be provided with information in the hands of central government.

The Standing Commission on Central–Local Relations would act as the guardian of the Charter, reporting publicly on threats to its provisions from any source, and thus alerting local and central government, MPs and Peers, to possible constitutional changes which might otherwise be overlooked.

What is required immediately is for the local authority associations jointly to establish a working-party to draw up a draft Charter, and to initiate a debate about its contents and the composition and role of the commission. If local government is not prepared to defend itself by taking such positive steps, the centre will continue to whittle away the powers of local authorities until people will suddenly wake up and realise that local government has become merely local administration.

Three questions may be raised against our proposal: whether it is possible in a country with an unwritten constitution; whether it would lead to more recourse to the courts; and whether it would limit local government.

Our Charter is compatible with parliamentary sovereignty and an unwritten constitution. Parliament would enact a Statute embodying the provisions of the Charter. It would contain a statement that Parliament assumed that future governments would follow these provisions unless Parliament expressly stated they were not to be obeyed. Therefore, if a government wished to act in breach of the provisions they would have to obtain fresh legislation, or be liable to challenge in the courts. Thus any attack on the constitutional rights of local authorities would be more explicitly recognised than at present. There could be more recourse to the courts, if the government acted against the Charter. But the courts would be acting in defence of local government's constitutional rights. They should not be viewed simply as extensions of central government.

The very fact that the government rejected in October 1982 the Draft for Local Self Government prepared by the Conference of Local and Regional Authorities of Europe (a separate but similar initiative to our proposal) shows that it realises that such a document would be a constraint more on its own interventions than on local autonomy.

14 The Case for Local Authority Control in the Government of Health

(with David Regan)

Introduction

This chapter sets the case for the transfer of the functions of the National Health Service (henceforth NHS) from health authorities to local authorities. That change could and would imply further change, but the case for the change itself is the subject of this chapter.

The case for the NHS being placed under local government rests upon the case for control at local level by an *elected* as opposed to an *appointed* body and for the NHS being made the responsibility of an authority carrying out a *wide range* of community services as opposed to one responsible for *one* service (or, more accurately, a *closely related* group of services). Both sets of differences have to be explored.

Election or Appointment

The NHS is controlled by a system of appointed boards. Their organisation differs somewhat between the four parts of the United Kingdom and has recently been altered. On 1 January 1982 there were in Scotland fifteen Health Boards, in Northern Ireland four Health and Social Services Boards, in Wales eight Area Health Authorities and in England a two-tier arrangement of fourteen Regional Health Authorities and ninety Area Health Authorities. (Henceforth all are referred to as 'health authorities'.) Besides the health authorities the NHS also had a managerial organisation at district and institutional levels.

Mrs Thatcher's Conservative government took office in 1979 with a commitment to streamline this structure. After considering the Report of the Royal Commission on the NHS which appeared in July 1979 the government issued a consultative paper, *Patients First* (Department of Health and Social Security/Welsh Office, 1979). The central proposal was the abolition of the Area Health Authorities in England and the transformation of the district management organisations into District Health Authorities. In Wales it was proposed that the much smaller Area Health Authorities remain but that the district management structure be swept away. A consultative paper for Scotland proposed similarly that the district management structure be abolished there. Following discussions with the interested parties the government announced its adherence to these proposals in a statement to Parliament in July 1980.

The English Regional Health Authorities were instructed to suggest the number and boundaries of District Health Authorities to replace the Area Health Authorities in their regions. The Welsh Area Health Authorities and the Scottish Health Boards were instructed to put forward new management proposals to replace their districts. Throughout 1981 these schemes and proposals were considered, perhaps amended and approved by the government. The new NHS structure, with in England 180–200 District Health Authorities (instead of ninety Area Health Authorities), came into operation in 1982.

Despite the variations within the UK and despite the current changes the common feature of all the health authorities remains that they are governed by a board of appointed laymen. Most health authority members are appointed respectively by the Secretaries of State for Scotland, Northern Ireland, Wales and the Social Services, taking into account nominations from local authorities, medical and allied professions, voluntary bodies and other organisations. The Welsh Area Health Authorities have one third, and the English District Health Authorities one quarter, of their membership directly appointed by the local authorities. In the English District Health Authorities alone the remaining members save for the chairmen are appointed by the Regional Health Authorities not the Secretary of State directly.

These complexities do not affect the central principle that the membership is in every case entirely appointive. The health authorities also employ administrative, medical and other staff, but authority over this officer structure is in every case given to a governing body of lay appointees.

There are other models for the government of public services. Three such models will be considered: the ministerial model, the local authority model and the nationalised industry model.

The minister as a full-time politician heads a department. The department acts in the name of the minister. Within that department there is a hierarchical structure giving expression to the direct responsibility of the officers to the minister. That direct responsibility is uninterrupted by boards, appointed or elected, claiming their own basis of authority. Authority derives from the minister who is himself a member of the government responsible to Parliament.

The local authority is an alternative model with some similarity to the health authority. It operates at a local level. It has a governing body of laymen. They are, however, not appointed but elected. Beneath the council is an officer structure, whose responsibility is normally through a committee to the council.

The nationalised industry (when a public corporation) again has a structure which has some similarities to that of the health authority. It has an officer structure, responsible to a governing board appointed by the government. It is usually a paid board composed mainly of full-time officials. Unlike the health authority it is better regarded as composed of the heads of the officer structure, constituted collectively as the governing body, rather than as an entity separate from the officers. The board is responsible to the minister for achieving certain financial targets. The basis for accountability is thus commercial and technical, which the constitution of the board reflects.

The model used in the health authority differs from these models. The principal difference from the local authority model lies in the difference between election and appointment. The principal difference from the nationalised industry model lies in the difference between a board of full-time officials and a board of laymen. From these differences derive differences in accountability.

The difference between the health authority model and the ministerial model is more complex. On the one hand the four Secretaries of State are directly responsible for the NHS. They are statutorily charged with the duty of providing the medical and allied services. On the other hand their duties are not carried out by civil servants as in the direct ministerial model. Instead the Secretaries of State delegate their responsibilities to the subordinate health authorities which in turn employ staff. The health authorities' staff are not directly responsible to the Secretaries of State. The members of the health authorities are, however, directly these ministers' agents.

It would be idle to pretend that most government institutions conform to three simple models. There has been a growing tendency to modify these forms and to set up new institutions with mixed characteristics. Nevertheless the organisation of the NHS is particularly unusual. McLachlan (1979) went so far as to describe it as a 'departure from traditional democratic modes'. He explained:

It was the first public institution of any size concerned with a welfare service universally available in which a different kind of democracy from that traditionally understood was introduced by a form of direct delegation from a Minister to chosen individuals representing a wide sweep of special and professional interests, but because of an intricate consultation process, where several inter-relating responsibilities were left vague.

This ambiguity of NHS organisation is made even more opaque by the existence of organs of public consultation and review. The day-to-day running of the NHS is delegated to the health authorities whose members are in the main appointed by the Secretaries of State themselves. At the local level there are also, however, community health councils (in England and Wales), local health councils (in Scotland) and district committees (in Northern Ireland). These too are entirely appointed bodies. They have no executive functions but are designed to act as forums of public opinion and channels of public complaints. Their role is returned to below.

The structure of the NHS provokes the fundamental question: 'What is the rationale for the appointed health authorities?' On the one hand by their existence they break the direct line of responsibility of health authority staff to the appropriate minister. Yet on the other hand they do not have the same status as the governing bodies of local authorities and nationalised industries whose rationale is, in form at least, relatively clear. Moreover, even as community representatives they are challenged by the community health councils (and their Scottish and Ulster equivalents). What then is the point of these bodies of appointed laymen in the health service?

In Search of a Rationale – Accountability

A public service in a liberal democracy should be so organised as to permit clear accountability for decisions taken. Is this value served by the appointed health authorities? Usually accountability is promoted by making public executives answerable to elected representatives. As presently constituted democratic accountability is entirely funnelled through the *top* of the NHS. Only the four Secretaries of State are directly responsible to an elected assembly, Parliament itself.

None of the subordinate health agencies is directly answerable. Complete responsibility for the running of the whole system rests upon the four Secretaries of State. On any NHS matter, even the most detailed, the appropriate Secretary of State (or his or her ministerial colleague or officials) has to respond to MPs' letters, answer Parliamentary Questions, reply to adjournment debates, appear before select committees, and in every other way account for his or her stewardship to Parliament. Formally the Secretaries of State cannot escape accountability for everything; the subordinate health agencies cannot accept it for anything.

This centralisation of accountability has three consequences. In the first place it means that there is in practice little effective accountability. Whatever the formal position, neither the Secretaries of State nor Parliament have the time or resources to provide more than partial, selective and spasmodic accountability. In the words of the Royal Commission on the NHS which reported in 1979, 'detailed ministerial accountability for the NHS is largely a constitutional fiction' (para. 19.2).

The second consequence is that the *attempt* to provide comprehensive accountability, no matter how inevitably limited in reality, is a cause of administrative and political congestion in the central departments concerned. The common Parkinsonian outcome is not just delay and confusion but preoccupation with minutiae at the expense of the significant. According to a former minister of state at the Department of Health and Social Security, 'The department has become bogged down in detailed administration covering day-to-day management that has been sucked in by the parliamentary process. The answerability of Ministers to Parliament may have given the semblance of control, but on some major aspects of health care there has been little central direction or control' (Owen, 1976, p. 7). The Royal Commission concluded, 'It seems to us that the fact that the Secretary of State and his chief official are answerable for the NHS in detail distorts the relationship between the NHS and health authorities. It encourages central involvement in matters that would be better left to the authorities' (1979, para. 19.23).

A third consequence is that the role of the members of subordinate health authorities is likely to be unsatisfactory. The findings of the Brunel University team, commissioned by the Royal Commission to study the working of the NHS, on the whole substantiated this hypothesis. They noted both that 'The great majority of respondents at all levels either felt that the impact [of members of health authorities] was weak or recorded no comment at all about members' and that this corresponded 'with members' own belief that they had no real opportunity to get a grip of the system' (Royal Commission on the NHS, 1978a, para. 10.13). The Brunel team were careful not to attribute this lack of impact solely to the structure of the NHS (1978a, paras 10.2–10.12). Nevertheless it is clear that the members lack a clear basis of authority and that if they wield substantial influence it is because of the chance of personality or other individual circumstances. Indeed the Brunel University team's case study of two areas where the members set up committees of inquiry into complaints and incidents showed that these arrangements aroused considerable staff resentment (1978a, pp. 187–217). In any case members are likely to be increasingly deprived even of this role by the Health Service Commissioner. The Warwick University team, commissioned to study the financial management of the NHS, found that the role of health authority members was even more constricted than before reorganisation and that this limitation was partly to blame for the inadequacies of monitoring (Royal Commission on the NHS, 1978b, paras. C9, 8, D29.1).

The untoward consequences of centralised accountability seem to have entirely escaped the DHSS when drawing up their 1972 *Management Arrangements for the Reorganised National Health Service* ('Grey Book') (Department of Health and Social Security, 1972b). Instead they formulated a principle which must take any number of prizes for opacity. 'Delegation downwards should be matched with accountability upwards' (1972b, p. 10). If this dictum has any meaning it could only prescribe that the subordinate health authorities enjoy power without responsibility (a recipe, if we are to believe Stanley Baldwin, for harlotry). Yet the research teams showed that the *members* of these agencies wielded very little power. In short, the health authorities do not serve the interests of accountability in the NHS; they tend to obfuscate it.

In Search of a Rationale – Management

In the consultative papers in which the original proposals for NHS reorganisation were set out, stress was laid on the management role of the health authorities and on the management abilities that would be sought in authority members. Thus in the 1968 Green Paper the role of the lay members was envisaged as 'the highly responsible and exacting task of making sound policy decisions to secure the efficient allocation and management of resources in the light of their knowledge of the needs of the service and of local affairs' (Ministry of Health, 1968, para. 57). Here, too, is Sir Keith Joseph's emphasis from his *Consultative Document* (Department of Health and Social Security, 1971, p. 2): 'The success of the proposals will indeed, in a general sense, depend on the quality of management. The Health Service is one of the country's largest enterprises, in terms of money spent, staff employed and facilities required. It cannot prosper without managerial skill.'

In the White Paper a year later the emphasis was subtly different:

> In general terms members [of health authorities] will have two interacting sets of responsibilities: the supervision of the creation and development by their chief officers of policies in response to changing needs; and the overseeing of standards of performance, both in quantity and quality. They will need ability to give guidance and direction on policies to their *chief officers charged*

with the management of the service (Department of Health and
Social Security, 1972a, para. 93) [our italics].

Management does not provide an adequate rationale for the health
authorities. It is hard to see why groups of part-time laymen should be
required to introduce management ability. Indeed they interrupt the
direct lines of management responsibility running from the
Secretaries of State to the health service employees. It would be easier
to justify focusing on the management ability of the full-time officials
themselves, as the 1972 White Paper hinted.

It is hardly surprising that there has been little emphasis in practice
on the management abilities of the members of health authorities.
The report of the Brunel team for the Royal Commission on the NHS
(1978a) clearly found little general stress on the management role of
the authority members; indeed the one authority in which they found
such stress was felt to require explanation (para. 10.4). The
components of the members' task as seen by officers were described as:

(a)   the monitoring of the activities of the Regional and Area
       Teams of Officers and District Management Teams who
       should be accountable to members. This was variously
       expressed as a watchdog or monitoring or a policeman role
       and was advocated by both members and staff;
(b)   final responsibility for planning (though this was sometimes
       thought to be too complex for members);
(c)   responsibility for specific major issues such as decisions on
       whether to close hospitals;
(d)   acting as a catalyst of public opinion and then arbitrating
       between the professionals in the service and public demand.
       They should apply common sense criteria to complex
       problems. They should be able to balance the lay counterview
       against that of the professional. (1978a, para. 10.3).

These are the components of the task as they have emerged in
practice. They do not add up to a very clear role, certainly not
management; nor do they in themselves constitute a rationale for the
appointed boards.

In Search of a Rationale – an Analytical Model

It is difficult to provide a cogent justification for the *existing* health
authorities either on grounds of representation and accountability or
on grounds of management. To discover what might be a rationale of
any kind of health authority it is necessary to analyse the structural
requirements of the NHS.

The NHS is a large, complex community service. Size, complexity and community focus are features which suggest a rationale for a system that maintains a national service while creating within it points of decision-making that have, to a degree, independent authority. Many would readily see the arguments for a national service in achieving and maintaining national standards of access and service. What requires justification is the need for points of authoritative decision-making at the local level.

Large organisational structures require to be broken down if they are not to be overwhelmed by their own weight. This argument of the dis-economies of scale suggests that, unless authoritative decision-making can be set lower down in the organisation, too many decisions reach the centre and initiative is curbed.

Complex services are difficult to govern and hard to understand. There are no known and pre-determined solutions for many of the problems faced by such services. There has to be an authoritative basis for independent action to deal with problems which cannot be governed by uniform, national, pre-determined rules. Complexity cannot be embraced within the simplification necessary for national rules for uniformity. The justification goes deeper. In a service facing complex problems with uncertain knowledge, learning can develop through difference and the capacity to learn from such differences. An authoritative basis for independent action at local level, within a set national framework, provides the capacity for difference and for learning from that difference. A service which aims directly to serve the local *community* has to be responsive to the needs of that community and also to its differences. This argument is again a justification for an authoritative basis for independent action at the local level, where needs can be identified and met.

For all these reasons the NHS requires a form of government which permits and encourages a variety of response within it. We do not deny the need for a national framework of policy or for uniform rules at key points. It is an argument for both uniformity and difference, with a balance between them. This argument provides a rationale for a structure that combines ministerial responsibility with points of independent authoritative decision-making at local level. It may however be argued that it can be achieved without interrupting the direct line of departmental responsibility and that an officer structure can provide its own variety.

This approach fails to recognise how deep lies the principle of uniformity in our tradition of public administration. Within a normal departmental structure there is scope for some administrative initiative; but more is required. The health authorities have formal independent authority to allocate resources between different services and different areas, which are not mere administrative decisions. They involve in a social service value judgements between differing needs. In that respect health authorities are given a critical capacity for difference, within the national framework, for resource allocation.

The case made for the capacity for difference in the NHS is not an administrative case. Nor is it a professional case in the sense of the capacity for difference in professional approach. That case does not require to be made. The doctor in the NHS has the authority for independent action that goes with his or her professional status. The case made is a recognition that many of the decisions made in the NHS are socio-political decisions involving choice between different values.

The socio-political concerns of health authorities may be contrasted with those of nationalised industries. In theory at least the responsibilities of nationalised industries may be defined in commercial, financial and technical terms. Thus it is appropriate that their governing bodies be composed of full-time officials who are, broadly, heads of the staff structure. In practice even nationalised industries find it hard to avoid socio-political value judgements and for this reason some advocate a different system of government for them (Jones, 1977; Hanson, 1961). Since the very stuff of health administration involves these socio-political value judgements, *a fortiori* the nationalised industry model of government cannot be regarded as suitable.

The need for a capacity for diversity within national policy provides a rationale for the local governing bodies contained in the NHS. If that case is not accepted it is hard to see any adequate justification for the formal authority conceded to the existing health authorities. It would be better to adopt a clear-cut hierarchy of departmental responsibility. Any argument for an interruption in that hierarchy is an argument for at least limited diversity.

The ministerial model is likely to remain rejected precisely because the NHS would be thought over-restrained in a direct administrative hierarchy. A capacity for difference is valued. The rationale for local governing bodies in the NHS is that they would provide that capacity for diversity, if they constituted an authoritative basis for independent action within the limits set by national policy.

The Local Authority and the Health Authority Contrasted – Relationship with Central Government

The case against the appointed health authorities is that they do *not* in fact provide the authoritative basis for decision-making at local level required by that justification. For them to achieve effective action what is required is not merely formal authority, but felt legitimacy in the exercise of that authority.

The dilemma of the appointed board is that it lacks the legitimacy required for independent action. The health authority cannot be regarded as an independent authority with its own basis of accountability. Its legitimacy comes only from the fact of appointment which does not make it accountable independently from the minister to whom health authorities are directly or indirectly accountable. Nor as in the nationalised industry can accountability be defined in commercial and technical terms. The dilemma of the health authority is that neither the basis of appointment nor the system of accountability gives the legitimacy required for independent action.

The dilemma of legitimacy is no mere philosophical point. It reduces the health authorities' scope for independent action in practice. This point can be illustrated by comparing the health authority in action with the local authority in action. It is a proper comparison. Both health authority and local authorities are concerned with large, complex community services. Both have apparent formal authority for independent action within limits set by national policy. There is however a critical difference. The local authority has a clear local basis for independent authority – the fact of local election – which gives the authority felt legitimacy for independent action.

Differences in felt legitimacy and in formal accountability lead to differences in action, in the approach of central government and in response. Within limits local authorities are treated and behave as independent authorities in their own right. Health authorities are treated and behave as subordinate authorities. The difference can be seen at many points. Indeed the difference is written into the very structure of local government as opposed to that of the NHS.

In the government of health there is a clear hierarchy of authority. In England it runs from Department, through Regional Health Authority to District Health Authority. Such a hierarchy is unnecessary and inappropriate in local government. True there are two tiers in local government, but there is no hierarchy. County and district are each authorities in their own right.

The local authority has the right as an independent authority to determine its management structure and processes and it exercises that right. The Bains Report (1972) at the time of reorganisation made general recommendations about the management structure of local authorities and that guidance was followed by most, although not by all, local authorities. Even then there was no sense in which the Bains recommendations were intended to introduce a uniform pattern, and since the original structures were set up there has been change and adaptation leading to a variety of approaches. Thus some local authorities, which originally appointed a chief executive, have abolished the position. In others the chief executive originally appointed without a department has now been allocated a department. The formal management structures change and develop in a variety of ways in a variety of authorities – as one would expect of independent authorities, anxious to learn from their experience and to adapt their structure to the learning.

The position is different for the health authorities. The Grey Book (Department of Health and Social Security, 1972b), like the Bains Report, made recommendations for the organisation of the new authorities. It had, however, a very different flavour. The Bains Report was written as general guidance. The Grey Book provides detailed specification. For local authorities it was assumed there would be variety and difference. For health authorities a uniform pattern was encouraged; indeed was laid down. While local authorities' formal management structures have changed, so that there is no uniform pattern, health authorities' formal structures reflect imposed uniformity. Practice may vary more than form in health authorities, but form symbolises imposed uniformity. Some local authorities have abolished the position of chief executive. No health authority has created that position. The uniformity in formal structure is no accident; it is appropriate to a subordinate authority lacking the legitimacy for independent action, although it is questionable if such uniformity encourages the learning necessary for organisational effectiveness.

The issue goes far beyond the question of organisational structure. It is merely a symbol of a wider issue. What is involved is the whole relationship between centre and locality. It is marked by the number of circulars sent out by DHSS to health authorities, which is many times greater than the number sent out by DES to local education authorities. It is not merely the number but the range and detail of subjects covered. It is yet again the difference between an independent local authority subject to influence and control at key points and what must be regarded as a subordinate health authority thought to require instruction on endless detail.

The Local Authority and the Health Authority Contrasted – the Working Situation

Not merely in its relationship with central government is the difference between the elected authority and the appointed authority important. Election and appointment affect behaviour at the level of the authority itself. Election creates an active relationship between the councillor and his locality: appointment on the other hand creates no such relationship.

The governing body that is a local authority and the governing body that is a health authority differ. Both control in form if not in reality complex administrative machines. The administrative machine tends to look inward to its task. The governing body has the capacity to force the administrative system to look outward – at least occasionally. The governing body that is a local authority has an active relationship with the locality. The governing body that is a health authority has only the passive relationship of appointment; there are few pressures on its members to turn the capacity into reality.

The elected member may or may not differ from the appointed member in ability, in experience or in background. *The critical difference lies in the fact of election.* It gives the member an active relationship with the world outside the organisation. It gives the elected member a clearly understood independent basis of authority that the appointed member lacks. It creates a relationship of accountability. The officer structure is accountable to the council members in a local authority, who are again accountable to the electorate. What that accountability actually means in practice matters less than that accountability sanctioned by the fact of election is accepted. It may be a myth, but myths have been and are powerful motivators.

In a local authority the officer accepts the legitimacy of councillor control, because the councillor himself is accountable. In a health authority lines of accountability are confused. Formally the officers are accountable to the health authority. It itself is accountable, sometimes through intervening authorities, to the minister, but its very existence confuses the clear line of accountability that would exist in a departmental structure. The fact of local election opens up what can too easily be merely an administrative system. Councillors are known by the fact of elections. If not known by name, they are at least in principle identified. They are representatives. They receive complaints from their electorate. Members of a health authority are unknown in principle, in that they represent nobody. Their job is to set local or regional policy and allocate resources rather than to represent: but without a basis in representation they lack a basis from which to act.

The complainant opens up the system. Complaints are a critical element in the councillor's role. They provide an alternative information source to that provided within the administration. It is no accident if councillors look outward. They look at least occasionally towards their electorate. There is no reason why the appointed member should receive complaints from the public. The fact of election opens up debate within the authority to the public outside. It is at least implicitly to the electorate that an appeal is made. The debate over comprehensive education was paralleled by a debate in health over the district general hospital. The former was the subject of local political and public debate. In the latter the debate was largely enclosed within the world of health authorities.

A governing board has the role of challenging professional and technical judgement. Such judgements have their very proper role, but professional judgement can extend beyond its proper area of concern, as is discussed below. Professional knowledge and expertise are a source of legitimate power. They can only be challenged by an alternative source of legitimate power. An appointed member has a weak basis for challenge. Local election carries with it both the perceived authority and the felt legitimacy to challenge.

The local authority differs from the health authority in form and structure, in its relationship with central government and in the attitude and approach of its governing body. It is no accident. It derives from the difference between an elected and an appointed authority. The local authority has felt legitimacy in independent action and a basis for local accountability for that action. The health authority lacks the felt legitimacy for independent action at the local level and would have no basis for local accountability for that action.

A Diversion into Institutional Delusion

The weakness of a system of appointed members has been recognised by institutional forms designed to correct that weakness. Written into the institutions of the new health authorities were two approaches designed to give the government of health some of the characteristics of an elected authority. The first was the creation of community health councils and the second was the appointment of a number of members of the health authorities by local authorities. Neither succeeds in meeting the main weaknesses of the appointed agency because neither meets the critical point.

As Phillips (1980) has shown, these two devices represented different preferences by the two main political parties. The Labour government of 1966–70 promised to provide for public involvement in a reorganised NHS by appointing local representatives to the health authorities – see for instance Mr Richard Crossman's foreword to the 1970 Green Paper (Department of Health and Social Security, 1970). The Conservative government elected in 1970 disapproved, however, of large 'representative' health authorities and plumped instead for small 'managerial' ones – in the words of the 1972 White Paper 'small and capable membership' (Department of Health and Social Security, 1972a, para. 90). This provision had two effects: a large reduction in the lay membership of these authorities and the destruction of their local representative character. Accordingly the Conservative government felt obliged to create some form of representative mechanism outside the management structure – the Community Health Councils and their Scottish and Ulster equivalents. According to Phillips (1980, p. 60), the Community Health Councils were only a symbolic gesture in the direction of consumer representation and the Conservatives were not greatly interested in their effectiveness.

With Labour's return to power in 1974 there was a renewed emphasis on 'representative' health authorities. Regulations were amended to give one third of the membership to local authority representatives. Indeed in a Department paper *Democracy in the National Health Service* (Department of Health and Social Security, 1974, para. 5) Labour went so far as to assert that 'The Government do not accept that it is possible or desirable to make such a clear cut distinction between management of public services and representation of consumer interests and views'. Nevertheless the Labour government did not merge the Community Health Councils with the health authorities and they remain today as separate institutions. Even a suggestion that people be permitted to serve concurrently on Community Health Councils and health authorities was not proceeded with (Department of Health and Social Security, 1974, para. 19). They still cannot.

Community Health Councils are, therefore, based on the premise that one can separate representation from management and control. In itself this view is dubious. It is hard to see a meaningful role for a representative body which has no effective involvement in management decisions. Health authorities are obliged to consult Community Health Councils but not to carry out their wishes. In any case, however, Community Health Councils do not enjoy representative legitimacy themselves. They are composed not of elected but, like the health authorities, of appointed members. In essence, what has been done has been to set up one appointed body to be consulted by another appointed body. Awareness of the inadequate basis of the health authorities has led to the creation of inadequately based Community Health Councils. To such strange devices does the desire to avoid direct elected control lead.

The presence on health authorities of local government nominees also fails to give them an authoritative local basis for independent action. The members representing local authorities are not directly elected representatives, but only another variant of the appointed member. They are merely appointed by another body. The fact that they may be locally elected councillors does not alter that. It is not merely that they are in a minority on the authority and cannot thus assume responsibility for health. They were not *elected* to assume responsibility for health. The local authority to which they are elected has no direct responsibility for health. The local authority representatives have no more right to speak for the local community on health matters than the other appointed members. They do not provide a legitimate basis for authoritative decision-making at the local level. It is not even clear that they provide a basis for local accountability, since they are discouraged from representing local authority views.

Their role is ambiguous. Councillors cast in that role are uncertain of its implication. They are councillors, but in this context cannot behave like them. It is as a result more difficult for a local authority to fill places on a health authority than ever it was to fill places on a health committee. Their role on the latter was understood, but their role on the former is not. The lack of understanding is no accident; the role is in fact confused. Councillors do not carry democracy with them. They do not bring legitimacy and authority indirectly. They can only be regarded as responsible for that which they are elected to be responsible for. Beyond that they are merely appointed members – no better and no worse than the others.

In such institutional diversions the issue of election versus appointment cannot be evaded. They well illustrate that theoretical confusion can lead to practical nonsense, and what greater nonsense is there than that the same English or Welsh local authority appoints representatives to the District Health Authority, to the Community Health Council and to the Joint Consultative Committees. Governing body, watchdog and consultation machinery all have the same basis of appointment for part of their membership. Even Richard Crossman, one of the architects of the system, while not appreciating its theoretical absurdity, had qualms about its practical effect. He records in his diaries, 'What I hate is that this is dressing the thing up to look like local participation with in fact the decisions still being taken at the top' (Crossman, 1977, p. 607).

The Choice

If – and it is the critical condition – health authorities are meant to be a point of independent and authoritative decision-making at the local level in what is a complex community service, then these institutional diversions are indeed merely diversions. The simple answer is to make the local governing body in health directly responsible to the electorate. If health authorities are not meant to provide that authoritative basis for decision-making at the local level then it is difficult to see the justification for present health authorities.

A local governing body in health, directly responsible to the local electorate, can be achieved either by giving the responsibility for the health service to one of the tiers of local government or by creating a new elected health authority. Either solution would give the legitimacy required for independent action. Either solution would give a basis for local accountability. The members of the governing body would have the authority that comes with the fact of election. Either solution would provide an independent authority justified, within the framework set nationally, in independent action. Each would provide a basis on which the authority could legitimately meet local needs. Each would provide a basis for local experiment and the learning that goes with it. Each would meet the requirements for an authoritative basis for independent decision-making at the local level. Each would increase the capacity for difference within the government of health.

The key issue is whether that capacity for difference is sought. In institutions different purposes are sought and differing needs expressed. There are arguments for difference and arguments for uniformity in the government of health. There are many who would welcome local initiative and local action – as long as local initiative and local action result in the 'right' decision. An independent authority has the right, within whatever limits are set, to make a 'wrong' decision. If it has not that right, it has nothing. It is an agent not an independent authority. It is geared to uniformity.

The issue has to be faced. If the position is taken that the need for uniformity in health provision leaves no significant scope for independent action at the local level, then there is no case for a local elected authority for health. There then seems no case either for the present health authorities creating the illusion of independent action, but the reality of confusion in accountability. The answer lies in the departmental model with an officer structure clearly responsible to the minister without the confusion of intermediate lay boards. The departmental model would, if uniformity is the dominant value, be much more appropriate than the present structure.

Precisely because the ministerial model is associated with the case for uniformity, it must be rejected. There is a place for a measure of uniformity. Our system of government requires, however, both uniformity and difference. From difference comes experiment and learning. From difference in authority can come sensitivity to local difference in need. There is a healthy tension in our society between pressure for uniformity and pressure for difference. A system of government can encompass both if there is an independent local elected authority and a national government responsibility to control the framework within which the scope for independent action is set. The combination of the possibility of difference and the possibility of uniformity underlies other community services. The argument of this chapter is that complex community services require both. There is no case for an appointed local authority responsible for the government of health. It merely creates the illusion of an independent point of authority without the reality. There is a case for a local elected authority for health operating within a framework set by national government.

A further choice, however, has to be made. That choice lies between a multi-purpose elected authority responsible for a range of functions over and above health and an elected authority responsible for health alone.

Community Government or Functional Government

The choice between separate elected health authorities and making the NHS a responsibility of local government must depend upon a judgement as to the extent to which the NHS requires its own governmental system or should be an integral part of a wider system of community government. The choice is not clear-cut. On the one hand it will be generally accepted that health services are a significant and distinct group of services, requiring a measure of separate administration. On the other hand it will be recognised that health services have close links with other community services and that this connection should be reflected in the way they are administered.

The present structure emphasises the distinctiveness of the health services. The need for the integration of the health services themselves was emphasised when the structure was set up, but little emphasis was placed on the need to relate the health services to the general framework of community government. It was a divisive integration. The government of health was separated from the government of housing, the government of education and the government of social services. Integration of the health services could have been achieved *within* the main structure of community services. Instead the choice was made for a separate functional rather than a community perspective.

The functional perspective is important in government. Functional divides are necessary. The danger is that government may think in functional terms alone. The reorganisation of the NHS was a functional one heavily focused on the needs of the health services as traditionally defined. The result was a structure almost designed for isolation. It was not that anyone set out to design a structure to segregate the health services from local government services, rather that in designing the structure the functional perspective dominated at the expense of wider perspectives. The government of the health services is based upon different principles from the government of local authority services. Every different principle has erected another barrier, no matter how unintentionally. The main ones are:

1   The health authorities are governed by appointed boards, while local authorities are governed by an elected council;
2   The health authorities are totally dependent on a government grant, while local authorities have in addition their own independent source of finance;
3   Health authorities finance capital expenditure from grant while local authorities finance much capital expenditure from loans;
4   There is a hierarchy of authority in the government of health from district to region to central government, while in local government each authority is an independent authority in its own right;
5   The management structure of a health authority is based on a management team. There is no central point of authority. The management structure of a local authority can vary from authority to authority, but normally centres on a chief executive. Indeed the government rejected the Royal Commission's proposal that each authority should appoint a chief executive (Department of Health and Social Security/Welsh Office, 1979, para. 11);
6   Politics is accepted as legitimate in the working of local authorities and is increasingly the basis of election, while in health authorities the dominant ideology sees politics as alien to their working;
7   Local authorities are multi-purpose authorities, while health authorities can be regarded as single-purpose authorities;
8   The government's structural changes described earlier erect yet another barrier. The boundaries of the old English Area Health Authorities coincide (save in London) with those of local authorities. The new District Health Authorities will not necessarily follow local authority boundaries. These structural changes will weaken relationships between health authorities and local authorities, and represent 'a diminution of the priority accorded to collaboration' (Wistow and Webb, 1980, p. 28). The government are strangely inconsistent in this respect between different parts of the UK. In Scotland each health board's area coincides, save in Strathclyde, exactly with that of a regional or islands authority and it is not proposed to change this structure (see Scottish Home and Health Department, 1979). In Wales too the Area Health Authorities are coterminous with the counties.

Organisational boundaries matter. They represent barriers to communication and joint action. Problems tend to be seen in terms of that which lies within the organisation rather than without and action tends to be planned accordingly. The organisational boundaries can be overcome, but at a cost which increases the more sharply boundaries are drawn. Where different organising principles have been used to build organisations, different organisational systems develop, generating different organisational climates and the barriers become greater. Like does not speak easily to unlike.

To a local authority the region has little meaning. To a health authority the political culture of the local authority is alien. To a local authority the claim of the members of the health authority to represent the health needs of an area lacks the justification of election. Financial issues have different implications to the two different bodies. A chief executive whose support could be critical to joint action has no equivalent in the health authority.

To the organisational barriers have been added the professional. Members of a profession talk most easily to other members of the same profession. They have the capacity to communicate without too much regard for organisational boundaries. NHS reorganisation, by concentrating all those of the same profession in the same organisation, reinforced isolation in the government of health. The impact of NHS reorganisation was to isolate behind powerful organisational barriers the government of the health services. It was the separatist face of integration.

The government have proclaimed the need for collaboration. The 1977 Act says with all the formal certainty (and all the organisational unreality) of statute that health and local authority will collaborate. Yet collaboration has not easily been established, partly because it runs contrary to the main design of the structure. In structures built, however unintentionally, for separation, collaboration looks and normally is peripheral. In any case collaboration has not been a high priority for the government as is evidenced by the latest reforms in England.

That does not mean that effective collaboration is never possible. Organisational barriers may be overcome. The accident of a chairman of a health authority who is also leader of a local authority can provide a linking point. An individual excited by a possible innovation may breach organisational barriers. Past habits of working may have been carried forward into the new situation by, say, a former Medical Officer of Health. Established and understood procedures can be carried on, despite new barriers, precisely because they are established and understood. Nevertheless, if the argument of this paper is correct, collaboration will be limited because it runs against the main principles on which the reorganised structures were built. There will be particular initiatives in particular authorities, or in particular fields. Such initiatives can be encouraged, but that encouragement is against the background of structures that have divided the government of the NHS from the main structure of community government. These divisions can be overcome by effort, but the costs of that effort are greater the greater are the barriers. Such costs set the limits to collaboration.

Limited collaboration is not enough. It can leave room for collaboration where an enthusiast devotes time and effort to an innovation, but administrative systems cannot rely on enthusiasm. Limited collaboration can cope with identified needs, established practice and understood solutions. It is no accident that the Reports of the Collaboration Working Parties were able to lay down procedures for well understood relationships. The child health service can be maintained. Routine relationships between social services and the health services have been established in well understood areas. Yet many of the problems faced in community services require more than the routine of established relationships. The needs of the elderly and of the mentally-handicapped and mentally ill may require new initiatives involving a whole range of services.

The need for integrated planning has at least been recognised, although achievement within the divisive structure may be far from the need. A far wider range of needs relevant to health are but little recognised. The government of the NHS does not match the government of the health system, if by the latter is meant the forces in our society that determine the patterns of disease and health. It is not merely that critical responsibilities for occupational and for environmental health are outside the responsibilities of health authorities – although the NHS focus on treating the sick is a narrow one even in health terms. Nothing is said in *Patients First* about prevention and health promotion (Outer Circle Policy Unit, 1980, p. ii). The issue is wider, however, than health functions as traditionally defined. The government of the NHS cannot match the government of the health system, because the forces that influence the health system are governed as part of the wider system of community government. They are part of the health system but they are parts of other systems – housing, education, social services, town and country planning. All are part of the health system in that they have a critical influence on health, but they are predominantly parts of other systems. The government of these community services could never be part of the government of the NHS, but the government of the NHS could be part of the wider government of community services.

A health authority concerned to understand the forces in our society that influence health must reach out to many services beyond the health services. Not all will be local authority services but many will. In housing policies, in transportation policies, in education policies, in social policies and in planning policies, local authorities shape the environment of health. That has been but little understood because collaboration has followed pre-determined routines. Little thought has been given to the inter-relationship between the health service and the growing leisure and recreation function of local authorities. The pattern of leisure and recreation provision that is developing for families, for the middle-aged and for the elderly should be a matter of concern for health authorities.

The nature of the transportation system determines a pattern of stress as well as opportunity. The physical patterns of towns and cities, villages and suburbs is moulded in part by town and country planning. Alternative patterns of community life emerge. It is not a case of simple physical determination, but of inter-action between social and economic life and the physical pattern. Nor can health considerations be irrelevant to the planning of our local communities. Town and country planning builds patterns of living relevant to the health system.

There is a wider sense of community planning that is relevant to the health system. It is not about the imposition by government of predetermined plans upon a local community. It is about the recognition that government touches the community it governs at a myriad of points and in that touching moulds a pattern of living. It is about looking at the cumulative impact of government in relation to the problems, needs and wants of an area and identifying those issues where change is required. Those areas are likely to be areas that must bring together different services – and in particular the main community services – and that must include the health authorities.

It is not merely that the wide range of community services are critical to health, but that the health services can be critical to other community services and issues. Consider the problems of deprivation, whether analysed in terms of the inner city or more widely. Health deprivation should not be isolated in our understanding, nor the health services isolated in our strategy for deprivation.

The divide between health and local authorities stands as a barrier to the understanding of, and the strategy for meeting, the needs of local communities. This problem would not be overcome by the creation of a new elected authority for health alone, although that would go some way to overcoming the problem in as far as it brought closer together the organisational climate of local authority and health authority.

A *decisive* step to overcoming the problems would be to make the health services a direct responsibility of local authorities. On that basis moves to the integrated planning and management of community services would be possible. We do not suggest that there are never barriers to working between the different services of local authorities. Problems of joint working are not solved by simple organisational change alone. But the differences in organisational climate would be lessened. The barriers created by the very separateness of organisational procedures and structures would be removed.

The creation of a single authority opens up a wide range of new possible relationships between the different community services. It opens up the possibility of variety and experiment, which was not possible when different structures had to be matched. Variety is easier to obtain within organisations than between them. A local authority does not bring together *all* community services. There are other critical community services. It would be foolish to pretend that fragmentation and division would not still exist even within local government itself. Yet a local authority responsible for health and social services, for transportation and town and country planning and for education has a logic and a purpose in community government – a logic and a purpose that might be seen by the governed as well as by the government.

The case for the health services to be the responsibility of the elected local authority, rather than the responsibility of a separate elected health authority, rests upon the place of the health services in the pattern of community services.

The Argument Against

The case for the health services to become a responsibility of local government has been based on two arguments:

- that there should be a local elected authority responsible for the health services;
- that the health services should be set in the main fabric of community government.

This case is not likely to be easily accepted. This proposal was rejected by governments of both political parties before the last reorganisation, and was dismissed by the Royal Commission on the NHS (1979, para. 16.22), and by the present government in their latest consultative paper *Patients First* (Department of Health and Social Security/Welsh Office, 1979, para. 6). The argument against local government control of the NHS is based on two publicly stated considerations – the opposition of the medical professions to local government control and the inadequacy of local government revenues to finance the NHS. See, for instance, the Green Paper on the NHS (Department of Health and Social Security, 1970, p. 7).

Professional Attitudes

Spokesmen for the medical professions have often expressed their opposition to the transfer of the NHS to local government control. They made clear their hostility to such control in the 1940s when the NHS was being established (see Abel-Smith, 1964, p. 447) and were still expressing it to the Royal Commission on the NHS in 1979 (para. 16.20). While these spokesmen rarely if ever present a fully reasoned case, their opposition seems to be based partly on a fear that local authorities would infringe their 'clinical freedom' and partly on a desire to avoid party political controversy in the health services.

It can be demonstrated in several different ways that local authority control would not pose a threat to the 'clinical freedom' of the medical professionals. In the first place local authorities employ a host of non-medical professionals – teachers, lawyers, engineers, accountants, architects, social workers, and others – without apparently infringing their discretion on purely professional issues (their 'clinical freedom'). Secondly, until 1974 local authorities employed *medical* professionals too, yet there is no evidence that *their* clinical freedom atrophied. (From 1946 to 1974 the NHS was divided three ways – hospitals, practitioner services and community services – with the latter, embracing functions like maternity and child welfare, vaccination and immunisation and school health, left under local authority control.) Thirdly, medical resentment of local government control before 1946 was directed not so much at local politicians but at medical superintendents, themselves qualified doctors (Abel-Smith, 1964, p. 470). It is hard to avoid medical superintendents or their equivalents no matter how health services are organised.

The evidence does not, thus, substantiate a claim that the clinical discretion of medical professionals was, or would be, undermined by local authority control. Moreover, the medical professionals complain just as loudly about their lack of power under the present organisation of the NHS as they did forty or fifty years ago under local government. Mackenzie (1979, p. 181) for instance quotes the public assertion of a surgeon: 'You can take it we now have virtually no power in hospitals'.

One suspects that when doctors complain at their lack of power in the operation of health services it is often really in respect of political not clinical matters. Their complaints are often about financial allocations, the work practices of ancillary staff, the closure of hospitals and similar matters not for medical professionals alone to decide. They should be *involved* in these decisions on a consultative or participative basis but must accept that their views will not necessarily prevail. As with most professionals the medical often seek to expand the boundaries of professional discretion. It is well known that, say, military professionals sometimes chafe at the financial and policy constraints within which they have to operate. It is important for our political system, central and local, that professional discretion be confined to its proper sphere. It may have been unwise as Hastings (1966) claims for the government to cancel the TSR2 but it was rightly a decision for the government, not the RAF. Similarly society may or may not benefit from the phasing out of pay beds in hospitals and it was rightly not a decision for the doctors. In both cases it was legitimate that the politicians took professional views into account; nevertheless they were not matters to be left to professional discretion.

The survey conducted by the Brunel University team for the Royal Commission on the NHS found considerable evidence of low morale among health workers (1978a, paras 12.1–14.7). Moreover the Royal Commission noted that 'Nearly half the evidence submissions which mentioned low morale in the NHS were from doctors' (para. 12.4). As was pointed out, such demoralisation may plausibly be ascribed to a number of factors like new trade union militancy, increased public criticism and recent financial stringency, but discontent with the power professionals wield also plays its part. Yet the Brunel University team pointed to wide opportunity for the participation of clinicians in health service management (Royal Commission on the NHS, 1978a, paras 9.1–17). It seems clear that much of the frustration of medical professionals is a consequence of their seeking more power than is appropriate. Some commentators see doctors' power as already excessive in, for instance, health planning (Alaszewski and Vulliamy, 1980; Elcock and Haywood, 1980).

The borderline between professional and political matters is in practice blurred and the mutual impact of the one on the other is considerable. Nevertheless, professionals cannot be left to decide where the line is to be drawn. In an area of public provision like the health services the issues that have to be resolved are not just professional; they involve value choice. As such they are legitimate subjects for party political controversy. The Brunel University team noted the inevitable tension between individual clinical needs and overall management policies. They concluded that the conflict between *collective* assumptions like allocative justice and *individual* assumptions associated with good health care was an inevitable one which no structure or process could entirely resolve (Royal Comission on the NHS, 1978a, pp. 223–32).

Professional objections to local government control of the NHS are thus misguided. On the one hand it poses no peculiar threat to clinical freedom. On the other hand it would not 'import' party politics. Political control is not avoided in the present structure of the

NHS; nor should it be. Value conflict requires political resolution. The issue between the appointed board and the elected member turns not upon the need for, or absence of, political control but on the form it should take. A proposal for local elected control is a proposal for more than one point of political control as against a single point of political control. It is also about the recognition of the need for countervailing political forces which might benefit the health services and the professionals engaged in them.

Financial Resources and Decentralisation

The only other major argument put forward against local government control is the impossibility of local government finding resources to finance the NHS. This argument is only valid if it is assumed that, if the NHS were made the responsibility of local authorities, there would be no change in the resources available to them. Such an assumption is unrealistic.

At present local authorities have three main sources of finance, government grant, local taxes and fees and charges. In principle any of these sources of income could be changed to provide the necessary resources, but it is assumed for the purpose of this chapter that fees and charges are ruled out as a major new source of finance. That would be a change in the nature of the NHS outside the scope of this chapter. There is however no reason why the transfer of responsibility for the NHS to local authorities should necessarily alter the main source of finance for that service. The NHS could continue to be financed by grant, only the grant would be paid to the local authority. It could of course be argued that local authorities could and should finance some proportion of the NHS either from the rates or by the introduction of a new local tax.

There may or may not be arguments against the continuation of the finance of the NHS by grant. There may or may not be arguments against making grant a relatively higher percentage of local authority income. There may or may not be arguments against additional taxes for local authorities. All these issues have to be discussed. What is clear, however, is that local authorities could finance the NHS provided an appropriate adjustment were made to their resources. Merely to cite finance as a problem is to avoid the issue, not to settle it.

Finance is less important in itself than as a symbol of a deeper issue – namely how effectively centralised the NHS should be. Successive governments have dismissed proposals for the transfer of the NHS to local government on the two grounds discussed. They are not entirely bogus. Governments do not lightly antagonise the doctors or undertake major financial reorganisation. At a political meeting in 1970 to which no journalists were invited, Richard Crossman, then Secretary of State for the Social Services, records in his diaries: 'I explained why we couldn't put the Health Service under local government because I couldn't just destroy the compact Nye Bevan made in 1948 to give the consultants the key position' (Crossman, 1977, p. 817). Nevertheless, there can be little doubt that governments *prefer* the NHS to be highly centralised. It is so much more convenient in a service as expensive and potentially controversial not to have to face politically powerful subordinate agencies. Appointed health authorities are politically feeble and can usually be bullied into submission without great difficulty. The Secretary of State for the Social Services could dissolve Lambeth Area Health Authority within two months of taking office yet create no more than a minor political disturbance. The courts subsequently ruled the dissolution illegal but the government was caused only mild embarrassment. By contrast it was a major political operation for the government to proceed against Liliputian Clay Cross Urban District Council despite its prolonged and open defiance of the law.

It is likely that the civil servants, as opposed to the central politicians, also prefer a centralised NHS. To quote Crossman again: 'In the first session we discussed the Green Paper that Kenneth Robinson had put out, indicating, as I now know the Department really wanted, that the Health Service should be reorganised into some twenty huge areas run by sixteen oligarchs responsible to London' (Crossman, 1977, pp. 328–329).

The problem of finance could be met, it has been argued, by giving local authorities either sufficient grant or sufficient local tax resources to meet the needs of the NHS. It may, however, not be the problem of the source of finance but of the degree of control over its use by central government that is at stake. To give grants to local government for the NHS (or to give local governments new sources of taxation) gives local authorities more freedom than would be enjoyed by appointed health authorities given equivalent grants. This difference is in part because the local authority is a multi-purpose authority which can spend its resources on a variety of activities. It is also because, as has been argued, the local authority provides an independent authoritative basis for local decision-making within the national framework, and has the felt legitimacy to exercise that authority.

The second point is fundamental. If such an independent authoritative body is resisted by central government, then it is natural that that resistance is strongest on financial issues. The problem is not however financial; it is that the rationale set out earlier in the chapter as justifying an independent authority within a national framework is not accepted.

The NHS may well have suffered from the lack of independent, authoritative, local bodies. Between 1946 and 1974 two thirds of the NHS lacked such bodies and since then the whole NHS has been so deprived. There are grounds for believing that one consequence has been a poor level of investment in the NHS, even during the relatively balmy decades of the 1950s and 1960s. The appointed local health agencies might protest at being starved of funds but their protests could be ignored as carrying little political weight or legitimacy. Appointees who try to bite their appointors are apt to discover that their teeth are rubber. By throwing their weight against local government control therefore the medical professionals have denied the NHS the political muscle to challenge the central government. By so doing they may well have contributed to the weakness of the NHS and thus to their own frustrations.

Conclusions

In the NHS the rationale for the existing appointed health authorities is feeble. They contribute little to management, have no legitimate basis for representation and confuse accountability. Their supplementation with Community Health Councils only makes the confusion worse confounded.

The nationalised industry model would be inappropriate for the NHS to follow. The ministerial model is, however, suitable. If the NHS were run like a government department with lines of management and accountability running uninterrupted between ministers and NHS employees then it would provide a clear structural rationale and would have much to commend it. Such arrangements would destroy the case for any local health authorities. The grave drawback of the ministerial model is that it would push towards centralisation and uniformity a service so complex and changing as to cry out for substantial diversity. Alaszewski and Haywood (1980) criticise the inadequacy of innovation even in the present NHS; they blame negative central control, an over-dominant medical profession and managers who mediate between interests rather than make policy. Nevertheless they fail to see that without a structure embracing local points of independent, authoritative decision-making substantial diversity of provision cannot be ensured.

Local points of independent, authoritative decision-making necessitate elected health authorities. In a liberal democracy political power and legitimacy grow out of the barrel of a ballot box. To facilitate the co-ordinated provision of services the elected bodies responsible for health services should be the same as those responsible for so many other community services, that is the local authorities.

No one would claim that transfer to local government control would solve all the problems of the NHS. Such crude structural determinism is to be avoided; but so too is the alternative fallacy of denying any importance to structure. The provision of a public service can be profoundly affected for good or ill by its organisation. The contention of this chapter is that the existing organisation of the NHS is a serious handicap to its effective operation.

The change proposed is not minor. It would have a significant impact both on the NHS and on local government. The local authorities assuming responsibility for health would be massively enhanced as institutions of community government. A change of such moment might even justify some reconsideration of the structure of local government, if some elements in it were inimical to the provision of health services. Those who advocate gradual and limited change rather than another upheaval (like the Outer Circle Policy Unit, 1978) will no doubt be put off by these considerations. At the same time, if the structure of the NHS is fundamentally flawed, persisting with it basically unaltered also has implications which need to be considered.

The case made out in this chapter has rarely been stated. Any contrary case must not only argue against it but put forward an alternative. If the alternative is the existing system then it too must be set out on a reasoned basis. In all the publications, official and otherwise, concerned with the NHS it is hard to discover a well developed case for the existing system.

15 The Future of Local Government

A Fundamental Reorganisation Next Time

The issue of local government reorganisation is once again on the political agenda. It is being discussed by the Labour, Liberal and Social Democratic parties and, at least for the metropolitan areas, by the Conservative Party.

Local government reorganisation is on the agenda in part because of the weaknesses of the 1974 reorganisation, but also because of the impact on the working of local government of the continuing changes in central–local relations and in the financial conditions of local government. The very pattern of local government has been destabilised, not only by the particular changes but by the process of change itself. Indeed, the relationship between central and local government has been so destabilised by the continuing changes in the financial conditions under which authorities operate that the only prospect for responsible local government may well be a new settlement embedded in a new structural reorganisation.

Reorganisation imposes severe costs upon the working of local government. While it is taking place, the main attention of local government officers and councillors is drawn away from the services for which they are responsible to the problems of reorganisation. Perhaps even more important, most organisations depend upon informal patterns of working, both in their internal structure and in their relations with the public. Habits of working, attitudes and loyalties are built up over time by local authorities, but are easily swept aside by reorganisation. The past reorganisation may have destroyed more than was realised.

Reorganisation should not be lightly undertaken, but the need to strengthen local government now requires a further reorganisation. To restore local government to a strong position it is important to ensure that the new structure is geared to meet changes and challenge over the coming decades, and that it is clearly seen as the government of the local community, so that local loyalties can sustain it.

For that purpose reorganisation must be fundamental. This reorganisation:

1 Should not take as its starting point the functions that local government happens to have at the moment, but should consider

the whole range of functions by which a local community is governed, including those currently exercised by health authorities, water authorities, the Manpower Services Commission, central government departments and other public organisations;

2 Should not take as its starting point the working of local government in its present form, but should seek to make local government an instrument of learning, of response and of change, grounded in public acceptance;

3 Should not ignore the problems produced by the fragmentation of local community government, but should seek, as a prime requirement for local accountability, responsiveness and effective action, a comprehensive structure in which division of responsibility is minimised;

4 Should not deal with structure and functions in isolation from the resources with which those functions are carried out, but should ensure that the system of local government finance sustains local accountability;

5 Should not ignore the central–local relationship, but should establish stability in the relationship as a foundation for responsible and responsive decision-making at the local level;

6 Should not ignore the essential need for local accountability and responsiveness, but should establish these goals at the heart of the review, recognising that they may involve a new electoral process for local government.

These requirements are critical for a major reorganisation designed to establish local government on a stable basis, capable of tackling imaginatively and effectively the complex problems of society in the future.

The Functions of Local Government

In 1974 no consideration was given to the functions appropriate to local government. The Royal Commission on Local Government was restricted by its terms of reference to the existing functions of local government, and the White Papers prepared by both the Labour government in 1970 and the Conservative government in 1971 looked no further. Indeed, in 1974 the only significant change made in the functions of local government was the removal from local authorities of certain health and water responsibilities, which had been the subject of separate functional reviews. Such inquiries into particular functions are likely to result in recommendations for the separate government of each function, precisely because such a review is constituted to investigate one function in isolation. In 1974 the functions which happened to be part of local government at that time were reparcelled and shared out between the two new tiers of local government, except that the two functions subject to separate review were removed from local government.

Any new reorganisation must take as its starting point not the particular set of functions that local government happens to exercise when reorganisation takes place, but should consider what functions are appropriate to local government. The need is for a reorganisation that will consider both the whole system of local community government, covering the total complex of governing agencies which work within, and have an impact upon, local communities, as well as the place that local authorities can and should play within that system.

Two significant insights about local government should guide that consideration: one focuses on particular functions and the other on the inter-relationships between functions. The first is that local government is a means through which choices are made, and the second is that the choices are about priorities between many services.

Local government is an instrument for making local choice. To give a function to a local authority is to give it to a government body constituted for local choice. To assert that a local authority is constituted for local choice is not to deny that other public authorities have some capacity for choice. Choice is an element in any administrative act. The essential difference between a local authority and other agencies of government, be they local offices of departments of state or specially constituted appointed boards, is that the local authority is constituted for local choice about policy, expenditure and taxation. The fact of election legitimates that capacity for choice and gives the local authority the right and the responsibility to make a choice.

Local choice can be sensitive to local needs and local problems, and to the circumstances in which those needs and problems have to be met. Local choice can reflect values held by those responsible for decisions made by the local authority. Local choice can express local initiative and innovation. A function can and should be given to local government when a significant field for local choice can be defined. Local choice is important not merely to attain responsiveness to local needs and values but also as a source of the diversity that assists social learning. Local choice derives from the characteristic of a local authority as an elected authority, but local authorities have another characteristic which provides a criterion for the allocation of functions.

Local authorities carry out not one but many functions. They are able, therefore, to consider and plan for the interaction of their many services in dealing with the problems their communities face. They have to make a choice between the resources that they devote to different functions. They have to go far beyond decisions on how to use resources to meet a single main purpose, and make the difficult and demanding choice between, for example, education and the care of the aged – whether that choice is made explicitly or implicitly.

Our system of national government is organised around the functional principle. The emphasis is upon separate functions and not upon the inter-actions between them. Below the level of the Cabinet only at the level of a local authority does there exist the capacity to consider and appraise not one function but many. Local government is expressed in choices involving many functions. In considering the functions of local authorities it is important to consider them not as separate but as a set, and to explore the inter-relationships between them.

Recommendations

Our aim is to create new and powerful local authorities as the basic units of local community government. Local authorities would be strengthened as agencies of local community government if three major functions deeply embedded in the working of local communities and closely inter-related to other functions of local authorities were made their responsibility.

1 Local authorities should be given responsibility for the local government of health, taking over the responsibility of district health authorities.

   The case for the local government of health lies in the need for local choice, at present imperfectly expressed through appointed district health authorities which have formal authority for local choice but without the legitimacy that comes from the fact of election.

   The case for local choice in health is deeply embedded in the complexity of social learning. The government of health confronts complex problems, and for the solution of those problems learning is required. From the diversity of local choice social learning can the more readily advance.

   Further, the government of health is artificially separated in the present system of local community government from the government of education and of social services and indeed of other main local community services, such as housing. By a reintegration of the health services into the main stream of local community government, the potential of local community government to meet and to direct change will be significantly increased.

2　The training functions of the Manpower Services Commission should be transferred to local authorities.

　　The case for these functions being transferred lies directly in their inter-relationship with the existing education functions of local government. The recent growth of the training responsibilities of the Manpower Services Commission has led to dangerous divisions emerging in the government of education. Training and education need to be considered together.

3　The probation service is directly controlled by local authorities in Scotland, but not in England and Wales. Its close inter-relationship with social services suggests that the probation service should be made a direct responsibility of local authorities.

These are our main recommendations for the extension of the direct functions of local authorities. Other sets of functions should be considered, since they may be thought suitable for transfer to local government.

1　The remaining functions of the Manpower Services Commission should be considered for transfer to local authorities. There is a case for the transfer both of the work of job centres and of special programmes for the unemployed. The case for the transfer of the job centres is embedded in the concept of local community government. Local government with its concern for the local community can well encompass the matching of jobs to the unemployed. Its role as a provider of social opportunities to its citizens entails also the provision of employment opportunities.

　　We welcome the growing concern of local authorities with the pattern of employment, the needs of the unemployed and the state of the local economy. The transfer of responsibilities for job centres and of programmes for the unemployed to the local authority supports that concern.

　　In carrying out the functions of the Manpower Services Commission, the local authority would be at many points administering national programmes, but they have to be adapted to local circumstances which vary greatly with the pattern of employment and the nature of unemployment. There is a balance in the argument which we wish to see further debated.

2　There are a wide number of inspectorate functions that play a part in the government of local communities. Some are directly controlled by local government (e.g. by environmental health officers or by trading standards officers). Others, such as the factory inspectorate and the alkali inspectorate, are directly controlled by the Health and Safety Executive. In so far as their main function is to enforce uniform national standards, the case for local government control and hence for local choice is the more limited.

3   Social Security functions are clearly very important in the life of local communities, and officials administering them have access to important information about local conditions. Their main function is, however, administering uniform levels of national benefits, and thus local choice is limited.

4   The functions of the Water Authorities are a candidate for transfer. Local authorities often argue for the return of the functions that they carried out before reorganisation – water supply and sewage disposal.

Water authorities clearly play an important part in the operation of local communities, yet the argument for the restoration of their functions to local authorities is weakened by the requirements of water resource management. Rivers do not flow according to local authority boundaries and the argument for the management of the water cycle as a whole, rather than being fragmented between many local authorities, is compelling.

5   The distribution functions of gas and electricity authorities could be transferred back to local authorities as part of their role as representatives of the local community.

6   The police service could be made clearly and unambiguously the responsibility of local government. The presence of magistrates on police committees could still be provided for, and there could be a statutory provision protecting the operational independence of the Chief Constable.

There are many other functions of government which have to be reviewed as part of local community government, but apart from minor functions, the main responsibilities for direct transfer are those above. However, because a function should not be directly transferred to a local authority does not mean that the local authority need have no responsibility in relation to that function. We need to look at local authorities in a new way and not just as providers of services.

A New Conception of Local Government

Local authorities have been considered in the past as direct providers of services. To give a local authority responsibility for a function has been to give it responsibility for direct provision.

A local authority can, however, have responsibilities for a function even when it is not providing that function itself. Such responsibilities have not been widely developed in this country, but flow naturally from a concept of the local authority as the basic unit of local community government with a wide-ranging concern for its area and involvement in the many activities of government. This view does not require the local authority to have direct involvement in the activities of each and every activity of government, but it can have a role as representative of the consumer and of recipients of the services provided by other agencies, both public and private. Short of direct provision, local authority involvement in a service can take many different forms.

A local authority can be given a formal right of consultation on the activities of specified governmental agencies in its area. Where these bodies have statutory local consultative committees, the local authority should be given formal statutory responsibility for such consultative committees, even though they may include representatives of other organisations.

A local authority can be given statutory rights to require of non-elected governmental agencies a level of service above that normally provided and laid down nationally. This allocation of roles would recognise the responsibility of the governmental agency in their operations, but give to the local authority, perhaps in return for providing the finance, the right to require a different form of service or a different mode of operation. This provision would represent an extension to other services of arrangements made by local authorities for passenger transport.

A local authority can be given a formal right of inquiry into the activities of other government bodies in its area. Such a right would give expression to the concern of a local authority for its local area.

A local authority can also extend its direct provision of services to the local community in new and different ways. It might 'sell' to the private sector many of its services and professional expertise, in such fields as management techniques, auditing, accounting and financial control, legal advice, public relations, architectural and engineering skills, all of which may be especially valuable for small commercial, service and industrial concerns, unable to provide a full range of such facilities themselves. Local government enterprise can, thus, assist private enterprise.

A local authority as the representative body of the local community can act as the protector of its citizens in their capacity as consumers of privately-provided services. It can promote consumer rights by monitoring the private sector, disseminating information, investigating complaints and generally acting as the guardian of the welfare of consumers.

Finally, that general concern should be given expression in the conferment upon local authorities of a general competence to provide services and to carry out any function not specifically prohibited by law. Such a provision would remove present restrictions based on the *ultra vires* principle, and would thereby enable the local authority to respond through local initiative to the diverse problems and needs of its area and of the local community within it. It would encourage local authority enterprise and experiment.

What is being put forward is a very different conception of a local authority from that of a local authority as a provider of a collection of services congregated together by historical accident or for administrative convenience. It is the conception of a local authority with a wide-ranging responsibility and concern for the social, economic and physical well-being of its area and for those who live and work within it. Such a local authority with a capacity for local choice requires a new approach to the nature of its responsibilities. Local government would be local community government.

Summary

The local authority as the basic unit of local community government has a wide-ranging concern for its area. That requires:

1 A review of the functions of local community government, to determine those that should be the responsibility of local government.
2 A transfer to local authorities of responsibility for all or some of
    • the functions of district health authorities
    • the training functions of the Manpower Services Commission
    • the probation service.
3 Local authorities should be given a general competence to carry out all functions from which they are not specifically barred by law.
4 Local authorities should be given a right of inquiry into all government agencies, operating in their areas, which would also have placed upon them a statutory obligation to consult the local authority.
5 Local authorities should be given a general power to require from governmental agencies carrying out functions in their area a particular mode of operation or a particular form or level of service.
6 Local authorities as champions of the welfare of the local community should monitor the private sector and promote the interests of consumers.

The Basic Unit of Government

An objective in the system of local community government must be to overcome the fragmentation of the existing structure. The division between county and district, between local authority and health authority, between education service and Manpower Services Commission is a barrier to comprehensibility and hence to accountability. It also obstructs effective change in the response of local community government to emerging problems. Change now occurs easily only where such problems fall clearly within the boundaries of existing agencies. The complex of bodies, with different modes of election or appointment, and with different patterns of accountability, is a system that baffles the people and does not encourage understanding and participation.

A principle upon which the new structure of local community government should be based is that of comprehensibility. A basic unit is required capable of providing both the main functions of local government and a focus at which those functions can and should come together with other functions which although not the direct responsibility should nevertheless be the concern of local community government.

In determining the size and scale of that unit, regard must be had to the main functions involved, and not specialised elements in the functions, which can always be provided by co-operation between the units of local community government. Thus special schools or forms of residential care or even specialist advisers can be provided by joint action. Government should not be stood on its head by having its scale determined not by its main responsibilities but by its components' specialisms. Basic unit as a phrase is used deliberately and with a purpose. Basic units provide building blocks to be worked with, in a variety of ways, to meet different needs.

The basic units of community government could normally be about 150,000 to 500,000 – although in exceptional cases larger authorities might be created. In the metropolitan areas they can be based on the present metropolitan districts. In London they can be based upon the London boroughs or combinations of them, as in inner London where the area of the old LCC might usefully form the territory of a new unitary authority. In the shire areas they can be based on combinations of existing districts. At the end there will be between 100 and 200 local authorities as the basic units of local community government.

These local authorities would be the only elected authorities outside Parliament, and wherever possible the functions of local community government should be based upon them. These local authorities would be a focus of attention and a centre for action.

No other tier of government should be constituted between these local authorities and Parliament. Where functions of government have to be carried out over wider areas, that should normally be achieved through joint action by local authorities. Such joint action is never easily achieved, but it is easier to achieve between adjoining authorities each with its own responsibility for its own area than between two tiers of local government, each with some degree of responsibility for the same area, and it is easier between authorities of equal status rather than between those of unequal status.

Such necessity for joint action will not be required for the main activities of local authorities but only for specialised aspects. There is a mystique of scale, which rests upon little more than the perspective of those at the level of the centre unused to thinking on the scale of the local community. Basic units of local community government should be on a scale which enables most decisions of officers and councillors to be made about situations known and seen by at least some of those involved and not be turned into an abstract of the unknown and the unseen because it is remote.

The absence of any intermediate tier of elected government is critical to our argument, even if it is on the scale of the region. Such an intermediate tier of government weakens the comprehensibility of the system and diffuses accountability. A system of government in which functions lie either with central government or with local authorities is more comprehensible than one where another tier of government intervenes. Functions which are regarded as involving local choice should be given to the local authority. The remaining functions are appropriately the subject of national choice. It is difficult to see the rationale of functions being made the subject of regional choice. The functions that the advocates of regionalism are often concerned about should be removed from the uniformity of centralism and handed to local government for local choice or for their joint action.

At the regional level many decisions made by officers or elected members would inevitably be decisions about situations unknown. Decision-making at regional level cannot be part of the fabric of local community government. Regional government shares many of the attributes of central decision-making, and its advocates are often centralists at heart, unwilling for government to be brought close to those affected by its decisions.

The weakness of the regional level is that it will be an intermediate tier of government. There is no rationale for such a tier being given major direct responsibilities. Most functions can be provided by the basic units of local community government, or where national considerations are raised by the national government. Regional government will inevitably be a tier weakening responsibility at the basic unit of local community government, or a stage in the process of distributing resources (a stage that could easily be left out) or a duplication of national government.

If the future system of government is to be based on a strong level of local community government the basic unit should not be weakened by an intermediate tier, for what we propose is a major simplification of the governmental system. We seek a focusing of responsibility, a clarity in accountability and an increased capacity for change.

The system proposed is based on central government being responsible to Parliament, and a new and powerful set of local authorities as the basic units of local community government. These foci should be the bases of public accountability, to which other agencies of government should be answerable.

This concept of the system of government makes yet more critical the relationship between these two centres of elected power. The concept of local community government put forward here is of the basic unit of local community government having a clear responsibility, a wide range of functions, and the resources to carry out these functions.

A much clearer separation and responsibility between central and local government is implied, with the main responsibility of central government being to:

• provide, maintain and review the statutory framework within which local authorities operate – central government should act with and through the authority of Parliament in setting the conditions for responsible local government;
• provide the resources necessary for equalisation of resources between local authorities and exercise control over borrowing by local government;
• assist the learning process, made possible by the existence of this system of local community government, through the spreading of information from authority to authority.

The responsibility of local authorities if established on this basis should not suffer erosion over time. The relationship between local authorities on the one hand and central government and Parliament on the other should be laid down in a Charter of Rights, the maintenance of which should be the responsibility of a Standing Royal Commission which should monitor the relationship and report to Parliament and to the public generally, both annually and when any specific change is proposed. In this way any change in central–local relationships will have to be made explicitly with the possibility of a public debate on the consequences.

Summary

The proposal put forward in this chapter is a major simplification of the structure of government with the creation of between 150 and 200 unitary local authorities as the basic units of local community government and the only elected authorities outside Parliament.

A New Basis for Local Government Finance

The case for a new system of local government finance has been made many times – not least in the Report of the Layfield Committee on Local Government Finance (1976, Cmnd 6453). Resistance lies in the centre. The recommendations of the Layfield Report were virtually ignored by the Labour government of 1974–9. The Conservative government's Green Paper on *Alternatives to Domestic Rates* (Secretaries of State for the Environment, for Scotland and for Wales, 1981) has produced no solution to the problems of local government finance. Yet solutions have been available. What has been lacking is political will to put those solutions into practice.

In a new reorganisation this issue would become critical. There is no value in another reorganisation that repeats the errors of 1974, a reorganisation made without regard to the financial base. As the basic units of local community government it is critical that local authorities have financial resources adequate to the range of functions with which they are charged. If the local authority is to be responsible for its expenditure decisions to its electorate and to be accountable to them, then it should itself have the responsibility for raising the majority of its own revenue from its own electorate.

There will be a need for grant, but it should normally be restricted to what is required for equalisation. The case for equalisation for differences in resources is clear. There is also a case for equalisation in respect of the need for expenditure, but it carries the danger that needs equalisation can involve central assessment and with it central government intervention. If equalisation for 'needs' is thought essential, then it should if possible be based on a scheme devised and operated by local government, through its Associations, rather than on a mechanism manipulated by the central government. This equalisation grant should represent not more than 30 per cent of revenue expenditure, net of fees and charges. By far the greater part of the revenue of the local authority should derive from local taxes determined by the local authority.

The taxes allocated to local authorities should be taxes that bear clearly upon the local electorate, encouraging both responsibility and accountability. The domestic rate is a sound local tax. It is clearly a local tax, visible to those who pay and difficult to evade. As a property tax, albeit a tax on the occupation of property, it is a legitimate tax. It bears clearly on local electors. The domestic rate should remain as one tax available to local authorities.

The non-domestic rate is, however, by no means as satisfactory as a local tax. Although as a tax on property it seems suitable as a local tax, it does not bear directly on local electors. The effective incidence of the tax is a subject of debate and discussion. But whether the tax is borne by the customer, by the landlord or by the shareholder, the tax does not necessarily bear on local electors. The non-domestic rate should cease to be a local tax and be transferred to central government, which can then deploy this tax alongside other taxes on industry. Local authorities can then extend direct charging to local commerce and industry for services provided.

Since the domestic rate is not likely to be capable of bearing significantly more of the expenditure of local government, local authorities require a new source of revenue. That source of revenue should bear on members of the local public who do not pay rates directly as well as upon those who do, thus increasing local accountability. The tax should be capable of raising sufficient revenue to

- replace some grant
- replace the non-domestic rates
- cover the cost of new functions given to local authorities.

The local income tax can meet these requirements. A local income tax would be paid by 10 million of the population who do not pay directly the domestic rates. It would bear clearly on the local electorate. Doubts have been cast on the administrative practicality of the local income tax, but experience in other countries and the work of the Layfield Committee shows that there are no insuperable problems in introducing a local income tax, provided the political will exists.

The system of local government finance would be based – over and above fees and charges – on

- domestic rates
- local income tax

as well as grant for equalisation purposes. A local authority would have the right to determine the level of the domestic rates and the level of the local income tax.

It is for consideration whether a local authority should have the right to move the burden of taxation between these taxes. There are difficulties in such freedom, but on balance we consider that it is appropriate for responsible local government to determine the relationship between its two taxes.

If domestic rates were maintained at their present level, local authorities, to reduce grant and to replace the non-domestic rates (as suggested), would have needed in 1982/3 to raise nearly £12 million in England and Wales, the equivalent of about 13p in the £ income tax. Central government could, because of reduction in grant and the transfer of the non-domestic rates, reduce national income tax by that amount.

This proposal does not take account of the anticipated increase in functions and in particular of the training functions of the Manpower Services Commission and of the Health Service. Responsibility for these services would add a further £6–£7 million (after allowing for NHS contributions in National Insurance, and assuming a 30 per cent grant), requiring about 7p in the £ local income tax. In effect, as the main provider of local social and community services, the local authority would levy the most significant part of the income tax. But that should not impose on the national government any insuperable problems of economic or fiscal management. It will still retain control over most taxes and can vary their rates, and that of the national income tax, to counterbalance the tax decisions of local authorities. It should be in control of local authority borrowing, thus ensuring that the public sector borrowing requirement, interest rates and the money supply are not disrupted unilaterally by local government. Local authorities will not be able to borrow to finance their current expenditure; and without recourse to deficit financing local authorities' decisions on expenditure financed out of local taxation will not inhibit the national government's responsibility of managing the economy.

Summary

The basic unit of local community government, the local authority, must be able to mobilise community resources to carry out its functions, to be responsible for their use and accountable for that use.

The key proposal is for the expenditure of the local authority to be financed by domestic rates and local income tax, with government grant reduced to the amount required for equalisation purposes and the non-domestic rate transferred to the national government.

The Representative Base of the Local Authority

The legitimacy of a local authority rests upon its electoral base, That base needs to be strengthened if local authorities are to fulfil the role of the basic unit of local community government constituted as an expression of local choice.

The wide range of functions, the comprehensible structure and genuine local financial accountability will each add meaning and importance to local elections. The issue has to be faced, however, as to whether the electoral base can be strengthened in other ways.

At present, the system of election at local level broadly follows the pattern at national level. Both are based on the majority, or first-past-the-post, system. The main difference between local authorities and the House of Commons, is that the local authority election is for a fixed defined term outside the determination of the local authority. There is no right of dissolution, although the existence of 'hung authorities' does raise the question of whether local authorities should be given such a right of dissolution.

In certain authorities (metropolitan districts and those shire districts that have so opted) elections of a third of the council take place every year except the fourth year, in which county elections are held. In other authorities the whole council stands for election every fourth year.

Irrespective of whether it is introduced in national elections, there is a case to be made for proportional representation in local elections. The arguments that are put forward at national level against proportional representation are mainly expressed as the dangers that come from too many parties and the need for clear majority government. That argument applies with less force to local government which has through its committee system modes of working that can accommodate the absence of overall majorities. In addition, the swings in local government elections have been pronounced, because they have been in part, although not entirely, determined by swings in national government popularity and unpopularity, which can be very sharp in mid-term. Such pronounced swings can lead to very marked changes in the number of seats held by a particular party on a local council.

However, the main case for proportional representation in local government is to strengthen the representative base by ensuring that the council is more genuinely representative of the votes cast in the elections. The council will be seen as more representative and will feel itself to have more legitimacy. Thus the introduction of proportional representation will increase its accountability and responsiveness to its local community.

The exact form of proportional representation must be an issue for close examination, but a single-transferrable vote system based on three-to-five-member electoral districts would, while achieving a more representative council, still maintain the link between the councillor and a local area – local government is already in many local authorities used to three-member wards. If such a system were introduced then all elections for the new local authorities should be on an all-in-all-out basis, and those elections should be held every three years, again increasing electoral accountability compared with the present four-year period.

A new reorganisation should not take for granted the electoral practice of past local authorities. Other possibilities should be considered to increase accountability to the local community:

1   The right of recall – a provision by which a specified proportion of the electorate can demand that a council should be subject to a new election;
2   The right of the council and of a specified proportion of the electorate to call a consultative referendum on an issue. While the referendum seen as an instrument of central control as in the 1982 Local Government Finance (No. 1) Bill was rightly resisted, its use as a consultative mechanism by local government should be encouraged;
3   The right of dissolution, conferring on a council or the mayor or chairman, the right to dissolve the council in order to hold a new election, if two motions, the equivalent of 'no-confidence' motions, were carried in a year.
4   The right of candidates to electoral publicity such as local radio or TV electoral broadcasts or the right to free post.

Summary

The main recommendation is for a local authority to be elected on the basis of proportional representation. This proposal has arisen from our concern to strengthen the representative base of community government, and to ensure that the council is responsive and accountable to the local inhabitants.

The Working of Local Authorities

The role envisaged for local authorities as the basic unit of local community government, capable of meeting emerging issues, is challenging. It will require a new adaptiveness in local authorities. Three directions of change can be plotted.

(a)   Not Merely a Service Provider

The local authority, its staff and its councillors, must look beyond the particular services provided to the wider role of the local authority in local community government. This perspective requires from local authorities an organisation that is constituted for more than the provision of services. It must review the issues and problems facing its local community. It will need staff sensitive to their local communities, capable of recognising changing situations and of seizing opportunities.

In the provision of services the local authority must be prepared to innovate. The issues raised by contracting out and the privatisation of local authority services have shown that there are other modes for providing services than the traditional direct provision of the service by the local authority itself. A local authority can discharge a particular function by use of a private contractor, but also by use of a public contractor, by worker or consumer co-operatives, by voluntary bodies or community groups. The breakthrough in perception needed is in the recognition that direct provision of local authority services is not required. A local authority can set objectives and targets for others to achieve in their provision of a service.

The local authority will need new types of staff, whose careers and experience go beyond local authorities and may encompass central government, the private sector or other agencies of government.

(b)   New Patterns of Decentralisation

As the local authority is itself an expression of decentralisation, so within itself it can give expression to new patterns of decentralisation. Within the local authority there can be the diversity that comes from an organisation committed to responsiveness to the variety of needs and values within its area.

The local authority can introduce forms of area management which recognise the need to bring together services for particular localities within its boundaries. The local authority can decentralise the management of schools, houses and other local units, allowing a much wider variety of approaches. The local authority can stimulate parish and neighbourhood councils, not as another layer of government, but as representative of sub-basic units and to act as their spokesmen.

(c)   The Local Authority and the Public

The local authority gains force as the basic unit of local community government if it can develop new patterns of relationship with the public.

The local authority can initiate 'state of the local community' reviews, in which all who live and work within the area of the authority are encouraged to state their concerns, not merely about the activities of the local authorities but of other public authorities too, and of the private sector. Public forums should be a part of the meeting of each council, committee and, in particular, of area committees. New forms of social monitoring and polling can identify problems and issues of public concern.

Summary

The key point is not to pre-determine the organisation or the working of the new local authorities, but to recognise that new patterns will be required to realise the opportunities created. The primacy of representative democracy will be maintained, but it will be supplemented by the provision of channels to enable the views of the public to be more directly considered by the elected members.

Conclusion

Many issues have been raised. Some have been proposed for debate and discussion only, but certain main recommendations are put forward as our conclusions:

1 A new reorganisation of local government is necessary.
2 This new reorganisation must be radical, to build a structure of government at local community level capable of learning, adapting and changing.
3 This objective requires strong local authorities, with functions and concerns going beyond present activities.
4 There should be between 100 and 200 unitary authorities as the basic units of local community government, and no other elected local or regional authorities performing the tasks of government.
5 There should be a Charter of Rights governing the relationship of local authorities and central government.
6 Local authorities should be given adequate sources of finance, including a local income tax, to enhance local accountability.
7 The electoral base of local government should be strengthened by the introduction of proportional representation.
8 New local authorities will require new patterns of working, in particular new modes of service delivery, new forms of decentralisation, and new relationships with the public.

Postscript June 1983

In the last few weeks before the June 1983 election the Cabinet desperately sought an alternative to the domestic rates. They failed, and in place of a previous (1974) commitment to the abolition of the domestic rates, they went into the election pledged to:

- the abolition of the Greater London Council and the six Metropolitan County Councils;
- the introduction of special powers for central government to limit rate increases in over-spending local authorities;
- the introduction of reserve general powers for central government to limit rate increases in all authorities.

The reason these proposals were introduced was not because in this year the degree of alleged over-spending by local authorities is greater than in other recent years. Indeed it is less. Certainly nobody could seriously argue that over-spending of under 4% creates serious economic problems. Nor obviously were they introduced as an alternative to the domestic rate.

The proposals leave untouched the fundamental issues of local government finance. They do not alter the dependence of local authorities for over three-quarters of their income on taxes that do not bear clearly on the local electorate, namely the non-domestic rate and national taxes that finance central grants. They do not strengthen but rather weaken the accountability of a local authority to its own electorate. They do not clarify the role of local government in our society, or provide it with a stable framework in which to operate.

There is no evidence that any of these proposals were deeply considered, that their implications were worked through or that there was consultation with those who work within local authorities or study their activities. The proposals were adopted in ill-considered haste as a means of meeting an immediate electoral problem – the writing of the party manifesto.

The issues involved are not minor. They concern the structure and working of local authorities, the only elected institutions within our country apart from the House of Commons itself. The issues involved in the proposals for central government to limit rate increases are of fundamental constitutional importance.

Local authorities in England and Wales have long had the right to determine their own level of expenditure and their own level of tax.

That feature is the basis on which our system of local government has been constituted. After all there is no point in local authorities having their own tax if they cannot use it to determine their own expenditure. Direct central government control destroys the purpose of having the tax. Decisions to overturn such a fundamental characteristic of our system of government should not be taken in haste and without consideration of the full implications.

The history of central-local relations from 1979 to 1983 was a record of over-hasty legislation, many of whose main provisions had to be withdrawn or revised. That four bills led to eight grant systems is evidence of instability that should provide a warning. Ill-considered legislation in a constitutional area can have unintended consequences.

The period shows how the pressures, inevitable when central government's and local authorities' areas of responsibility are confused, drive central government controls and powers once introduced into new uses, even though the possibilities of such uses were denied when the powers were first introduced. Therefore, it can be predicted that powers against a few over-spending authorities will in time come to be applied to more and more authorities as the pressures for central intervention intensify. Further, reserve powers will become actual powers, and set a regular annual limit to local government rate increases. The moment for sober consideration of such proposals is before the powers are obtained. Afterwards there is no hope of pause or alteration.

The danger is that governmental institutions are being weakened and eroded. Institutions are easily destroyed; they are much more difficult to build up. Change in institutions of government should be carefully considered.

It was reported in the press that before the manifesto was finalised the Secretary of State for the Environment, Tom King, opposed the proposals for the central government to determine rate levels, but his constitutional objections were defeated by the Treasury's insistence on controlling rates. Indeed it is said that because he seemed so uncommitted to the proposals, Mrs Thatcher after the election replaced him at Environment with Patrick Jenkin, who is thought to be ready to implement the manifesto.

The manifesto was published. The Government has been re-elected on the basis of that manifesto. It will be said that there is no choice. The Government is committed and must act in line with its mandate.

We do not accept that view. The issues involved are of such constitutional importance that a pause is required, so that all concerned, the Government, local authorities and the public, can consider the issues involved. The proposals were hurriedly constructed in the pre-election confusion and were not extensively discussed in the campaign. They featured hardly at all.

Given the way these proposals emerged, it would be irresponsible for the Government to be irrevocably committed to the destruction of the financial independence of local authorities by assuming control over local authorities' taxation decisions.

Central government has become entangled with local authorities in a seemingly endless conflict. There is another way of resolving the problems. The accountability of local authorities to their own electorate can be increased not weakened. A new tax – a local income tax – could be introduced to replace not the domestic rate, but government grant and the non-domestic rate, sharpening thereby the accountability of the council to its own electorate, and thus making it an ally, not an enemy, of the Government in the quest for economical use of resources.

We would not expect the Government to adopt such a proposal easily. The manifesto commitment stands as a barrier. And yet that possibility shows that there is another approach which should be considered. So far it has not been given serious attention by Government.

We believe that the solution both for a Government committed to, but not wishing to, destroy the traditional basis of local government, and for local authorities committed to, but with many not wishing to, oppose the central Government, is a pause for calm reflection.

We propose that a Royal Commission should be set up to consider the role of local government in our society, so that the issues may be probed in depth before irreversible action is taken.

This Commission would not take evidence over many years. The evidence is there. Commissions and Committees have gone over the ground many many times. Analyses have been carried out. What is now needed is a Commission that could review all this material and make recommendations within six months. A considered judgement is required.

Both central government and local authorities would benefit from such an inquiry. The alternative is hasty action, conflict and crisis, the destruction of local government and the over-loading of central government. We urge the considered way.

References

Abel-Smith, Brian (1964), *The Hospitals 1800–1948: A Study in Social Administration in England and Wales* (London: Heinemann).

Alaszewski, A., and Vulliamy, D. (1980), *Children in Liverpool: Who Cares* (University of Hull).

Alaszewski, A., and Haywood, S. (1980), *Crisis in the Health Service* (London: Croom Helm).

Bains Report (1972), *The New Local Authorities: Management and Structure*, Report of a Study Group under the chairmanship of M. A. Bains (London: HMSO).

Barnett, Joel (1982), *Inside the Treasury* (London: Andre Deutsch).

Chancellor of the Exchequer (1977), *The Government's Expenditure Plans*, Cmnd 6721 (London: HMSO).

Chancellor of the Exchequer (1981), *The Government's Expenditure Plans 1981–82 to 1983–84*, Cmnd 8175 (London: HMSO).

Chancellor of the Exchequer (1982), *The Government's Expenditure Plans 1982–83 to 1984–85*, Cmnd 8494 (London: HMSO).

Crossman, R. H. S. (1977), *The Diaries of a Cabinet Minister*, Vol. III, *Secretary of State for Social Services 1968–70* (London: Hamish Hamilton/Jonathan Cape).

Department of Health and Social Security (1970), *National Health Service: The Future Structure of the National Health Service*, Green Paper (London: HMSO).

Department of Health and Social Security (1971), *National Health Service Reorganisation: A Consultative Document* (London).

Department of Health and Social Security (1972a), *National Health Service Reorganisation: England*, White Paper, Cmnd 5055 (London: HMSO).

Department of Health and Social Security (1972b), *Management Arrangements for the Reorganised National Health Service* (Grey Book) (London: HMSO).

Department of Health and Social Security (1974), *Democracy in the National Health Service: Membership of Health Authorities* (London: HMSO).

Department of Health and Social Security/Welsh Office (1979), *Patients First*, Consultative Paper on the structure and management of the National Health Service in England and Wales (London: HMSO).

Elcock, H., and Haywood, S. (1980), *The Buck Stops Where? Decentralised Administration in the NHS* (University of Hull).

Elliott, Michael (1981), *The Role of Law in Central–Local Relations* (London: Social Science Research Council).

Hanson, A. H. (1961), *Parliament and Public Ownership* (London: Cassell).

Hastings, Stephen (1966), *The Murder of the TSR2* (London: Macdonald).

House of Commons Environment Committee (1982), *Enquiry into Methods of Financing Local Government in the Context of the Government's Green Paper, Cmnd 8449*, Second Report, HC (1981–82) 217 (London: HMSO).

House of Commons Expenditure Committee (1975), *The Motor Vehicle Industry*, Fourteenth Report, HC (1974–75) 617 (London: HMSO).

House of Commons Transport Committee (1982), *Transport in London*, Fifth Report, HC (1981–82) 127 (London: HMSO).

Jones, G. W. (1977), *Responsibility and Government*, Inaugural Lecture (London: London School of Economics).

Layfield Report (1976), *Local Government Finance*, Report of the Layfield Committee, Cmnd 6453 (London: HMSO).

Mackenzie, W. J. M. (1979), *Power and Responsibility in Health Care: The National Health Service as a political institution* (London: Oxford University Press).

McLachlan, Gordon (1979), 'Foreword' in Mackenzie (1979), *Power and Responsibility*.

Ministry of Health (1968), *National Health Service: The Administrative Structure of the Medical and Related Services: England and Wales*, Green Paper (London: HMSO).

Moss, L. (1980), *Some Attitudes Towards Government* (London: Birkbeck College).

Outer Circle Policy Unit (1978), *A New Perspective on the National Health Service* (London: Outer Circle Policy Unit).

Outer Circle Policy Unit (1980), *Health First: A Comment on Patients First* (London: Outer Circle Policy Unit).

Owen, David (1976), *In Sickness and in Health* (London: Quartet).

Phillips, David (1980), 'The creation of consultative councils in the NHS', *Public Administration*, Spring 1980, vol. 58.

Pliatzky, Sir Leo (1982), *Getting and Spending* (Oxford: Blackwell).

Raine, John (ed.) (1981), *In Defence of Local Government* (Birmingham University, Institute of Local Government Studies).

Royal Commission on the National Health Service (1978a), *The Working of the National Health Service, Research Paper Number 1* (a study by a team from the Department of Government, Brunel University) (London: HMSO).

Royal Commission on the National Health Service (1978b), *Management of Financial Resources in the National Health Service, Research Paper Number 2* (a report by a research team at the University of Warwick) (London: HMSO).

Royal Commission on the National Health Service (1979) (Chairman, Sir Alex Merrison), *Report*, Cmnd 7615 (London: HMSO).

Scottish Home and Health Department (1979), *Structure and Management of the NHS in Scotland* (Edinburgh: HMSO).

Secretaries of State for the Environment and for Wales (1977), *Local Government Finance*, Cmnd 6813 (London: HMSO).

Secretaries of State for the Environment, for Scotland and for Wales (1981), *Alternatives to Domestic Rates*, Cmnd 8449 (London: HMSO).

Wistow, Gerald, and Webb, Adrian (1980), *Patients First: One Step Backwards for Collaboration?* (Loughborough University).

Index